Aleksander Jedrosz • Susan Loxley • John Watts

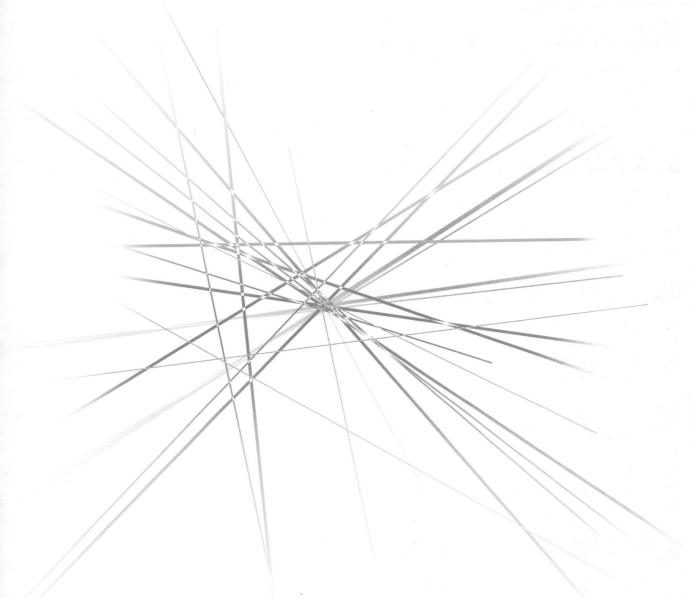

ESSENTIALS

EDEXCEL
GCSE Science
Revision Guide

Contents

How to Use This Guide

This revision guide has been written and developed to help you get the most out of your revision. This guide covers both Foundation and Higher Tier content.

HT Content that will only be tested on the Higher Tier papers appears in a pale yellow tinted box labelled with the **HT** symbol.

- The **coloured page headers** clearly identify the separate units, so that you can revise for each one separately: Unit B1 is red; Unit C1 is purple, and Unit P1 is blue.
- You'll find **key words** in a yellow box on each two-page spread. They are also highlighted in colour within the text. Higher Tier key words are highlighted in orange. Make sure you know and understand all these words before moving on!

- There's a **glossary** at the end of each topic. Each glossary contains the key words from throughout that topic so you can check any definitions you're unsure of.
- There are **practice questions** at the end of each topic so that you can test yourself on what you've just learned. (The answers are given on pages 120–123 so you can mark them yourself.) Please note that the practice questions don't necessarily reflect the type of questions you'll get in the exam. The practice questions are simply to test your knowledge on the information you've just read in the topic.
- The **tick boxes** on the contents page let you track your revision progress: simply put a tick in the box next to each topic when you're confident that you know it.
- Don't just read the guide – **learn actively**! Constantly test yourself without looking at the text.

Good luck with your exams!

How Science Works

How Science Works is an important requirement in the criteria for GCSE Science. It's a set of key concepts, relevant to all areas of science, concerned with the practices and procedures used to collect scientific evidence and the impact it has on society and your life. To reflect Edexcel's approach to How Science Works, and the way this element is taught in schools, these concepts are integrated with the scientific content throughout this guide.

Assessment

As a revision guide, this book focuses on the material that's externally assessed (i.e. tested under exam conditions). It doesn't cover the practical skills assessment and assessment activities, which are marked by your teacher.

There are several assessment routes available, which will include multiple-choice tests and structured question papers.

Environment

Food Chains

A **food chain** shows…

- the feeding relationship between living **organisms** in a habitat
- how energy and **biomass** are transferred when organisms feed.

Biomass is the total mass of organic material at each stage in the food chain.

All food chains start with green plants. They are the **producers**. An organism that eats another organism is called a **consumer**.

Grass
All food chains start with green plants. They are the **producers**.

Rabbit
This is a **herbivore** (plant eater).

Stoat
This is a **carnivore** (meat eater).

Fox
The fox is called a **top carnivore**, because nothing eats it.

Pyramids of Biomass

Energy enters a food chain from the Sun. Energy and biomass are lost at each stage in a food chain through…

- faeces (solid waste)
- movement energy
- heat energy (especially by birds and mammals).

So, only a small amount of energy and biomass is transferred to the next feeding level (i.e. the next consumer). This is shown in a **pyramid of biomass**.

Pyramids of biomass describe food chains **quantitatively** so they're more accurate than food chains and pyramids of numbers.

Energy

The fox gets the last tiny bit of energy left after all the others have had a share.

The stoats run around, mate, excrete, keep warm, etc. and pass on about $\frac{1}{10}$ of all the energy they got from the rabbits.

The rabbits run around, mate, excrete, keep warm, etc. and pass on about $\frac{1}{10}$ of all the energy they got from the grass.

The Sun is the energy source for all organisms, but only a fraction of the Sun's energy is actually captured in photosynthesis.

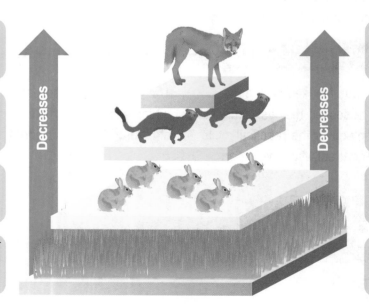

Biomass

The fox gets the biomass that remains to be passed on after all this!

The stoats lose quite a bit of biomass in droppings and urine.

The rabbits lose quite a lot of biomass in droppings and urine.

A lot of the biomass remains in the ground as the root system.

How Food Chains Affect You

If you went to the supermarket to buy a steak and a loaf of bread, you'd find that the steak is much more expensive than the loaf of bread. This is because the main ingredient in bread is wheat flour, and wheat is a producer. About 10% of the **energy** it absorbs is converted into food.

Steak comes from a cow, which is a consumer. Only 4% of the energy and biomass in the grass eaten by a cow is taken into its body (i.e. converted into steak).

This means a lot of grass is needed to provide enough energy for just two cows, from which only 0.2 tonnes of meat could be produced. But, if the farmer used the same land to produce wheat, he could produce 9.5 tonnes of grain.

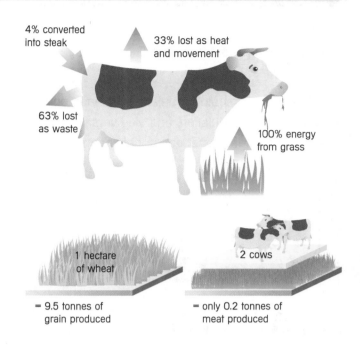

4% converted into steak

33% lost as heat and movement

63% lost as waste

100% energy from grass

1 hectare of wheat = 9.5 tonnes of grain produced

2 cows = only 0.2 tonnes of meat produced

Competition

Organisms in an **ecosystem compete** for **space**, **food** and **water**. The plants and animals that are best **adapted** to their **environment** are most likely to be successful: the plant with the deepest roots can reach water and nutrients that other plants can't, and the animal with the strongest legs is most likely to catch the prey. Successful organisms often exist in large numbers and may out-compete other **species**.

When there's plenty of food and water, a **population** will grow. But, **overcrowding** leads to disease and **competition** within the same species. When this happens, the population will decrease.

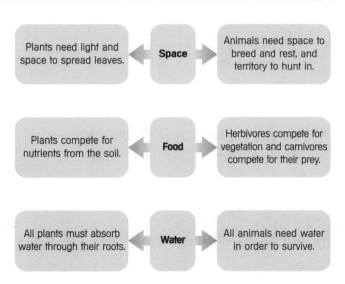

Plants need light and space to spread leaves. **Space** Animals need space to breed and rest, and territory to hunt in.

Plants compete for nutrients from the soil. **Food** Herbivores compete for vegetation and carnivores compete for their prey.

All plants must absorb water through their roots. **Water** All animals need water in order to survive.

Intra-species Competition

Intra-species competition is when members of the same species compete for a resource (e.g. food).

The strongest, healthiest and best adapted of the species has the best chance of survival.

Key Words

Adaptation • Biomass • Competition • Ecosystem • Environment • Food chain • Intra-species • Organism • Population • Quantitatively • Species

Environment

Predator–Prey Cycles

Predators are animals that kill and eat other animals. The animals that are killed and eaten are called **prey**.

The size of the predator population depends on the size of the prey population, and vice versa. This means there's **interdependence** between them.

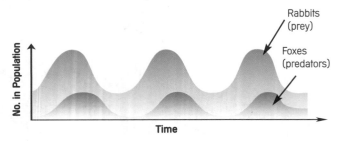

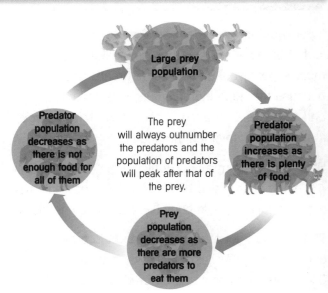

Large prey population

The prey will always outnumber the predators and the population of predators will peak after that of the prey.

Predator population increases as there is plenty of food

Prey population decreases as there are more predators to eat them

Predator population decreases as there is not enough food for all of them

Computer Models of Populations

Scientists use **computer models** to estimate population sizes. They enter data about…
- life expectancy
- reproductive rate
- food availability
- habitat
- predators.

By changing the data, scientists can predict what would happen to population sizes in different situations.

Advantages:
- Scientists can predict population sizes over many generations in just a few minutes.
- They can predict the effects of factors, such as climate change or disease, on a population.

Disadvantages:
- All the factors that could affect a population's size must be programmed into the computer.
- Too many assumptions might be made about the factors that affect a population's growth.

HT Human Activity and the Environment

Human activity directly affects the **environment**. For example, when we burn coal, a polluting gas called **sulphur dioxide** is produced. **Lichens** are sensitive to sulphur dioxide; even low levels can kill them.

The table shows how the population of lichens changes in relation to sulphur dioxide levels. When human activity affects the population size of one **species**, it affects the whole **food chain**.

Distance from Industrial Centre (km)	Sulphur Dioxide Levels (Arbitrary Units)	Number of Lichens Found
0	170	0
2	140	1
4	88	7
6	44	28
8	5	49

Changing Species

A species' **characteristics** can change over time.
There are three ways in which this can happen:

Method	Description	How it Happens
Natural selection	The basis of **Darwin's Theory of Evolution**: individuals with characteristics that make them better suited / adapted to their environment are more likely to survive and reproduce.	Naturally
Selective Breeding	Individuals with specific characteristics are selected and bred to produce offspring with desirable features.	Human intervention
Genetic Engineering	Genes (DNA) from one organism are implanted into another organism to introduce certain characteristics. They are **genetically modified**. The genes can be of the same species or different species.	Human intervention

Selective Breeding – Example

In the competitive farming industry, cattle need to be very efficient in order for the farm to make money. So farmers use selective breeding. This means **breeding** cattle to **specialise** in one of the following **characteristics**: beef production, milk quality or milk quantity. Cattle are **selected and bred** for one of these characteristics.

Most cows produce 5 gallons of milk but two in the herd produce 6 gallons. These two are used to breed from.

Key Words

**Characteristic • Genetic engineering •
Genetically modified • Interdependence •
Natural selection • Predator • Prey •
Selective breeding**

(HT) Genetic Engineering – Example

Soya is a very important food. But, the growing conditions needed for soya also encourage weeds.

The weeds can be killed using **herbicides**, but herbicides kill the soya plants too. So, soya can be genetically modified to resist the herbicide.

1. A herbicide-resistant weed is found.
2. The gene that's responsible for the resistance is identified and cut out using an enzyme.
3. The gene is transferred to the embryo soya plants.
4. The soya plants grow as genetically modified (GM) plants. They are resistant to the herbicide.

Environment

Farming Methods

There are two types of farming: **intensive** and **organic**. **Intensive farming** uses methods that produce large quantities of eggs, meat, crops, etc.

HT **Genetic engineering** is used in intensive farming to produce GM crops that...

- are resistant to herbicides, e.g. soya
- have a longer shelf-life, e.g. tomatoes
- are more appealing to buyers, e.g. vegetables that are a nicer colour or have a better flavour.

But the use of genetically modified crops raises ethical concerns such as...

- is it right to interfere with nature in this way?
- what are the long-term effects?

Organic farming uses organic methods that tend to produce smaller quantities of eggs, crops, etc. But organic farmers provide lots of space for the animals and produce as little pollution as possible.

Intensive farms...

- cost a lot to set up
- tend to specialise in one product
- need less land than organic farms
- use **fertilisers** and **pesticides**, which are cost-effective
- use machines to get the work done.

Organic farms...

- cost little to set up (but a lot to run)
- farm different crops and livestock
- need more land than intensive farms to produce the same volumes
- use **organic fertilisers** (which cost more)
- use manual labour to get the work done. (They are labour intensive.)

Because of this, products from organic farms usually cost more than products from intensive farms.

Evolution

The theory of **evolution** states that all living organisms developed from simple life forms.

Species **evolve** in order to become better **adapted** to their environment. Species that aren't well adapted become **extinct**.

The Fossil Record

Fossils are the remains of living organisms from millions of years ago. They're found in sedimentary rocks and provide evidence of evolution – they show the changes in a species over time.

The fossil record is incomplete because...

- many organisms have body parts that don't fossilise
- many fossils still haven't been discovered.

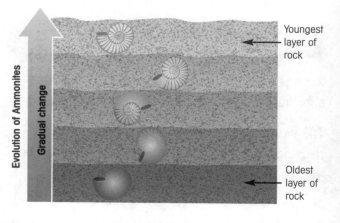

Evolution of Ammonites

Gradual change

Youngest layer of rock

Oldest layer of rock

Natural Selection

Evolution causes a species to change over time by natural selection. It may result in…

- changes within a species
- a new species altogether.

Evolution by **natural selection** follows this sequence:

1. Individuals in a population show **variation**.
2. Some individuals are killed due to **predation** and **competition**.
3. Better-adapted individuals **survive** and **breed**.
4. This is called survival of the fittest.
   The better-adapted **genes are passed on**.
5. Natural selection results in changes within a species and the formation of new species from genetic variations and mutations.
6. Over generations, the effects of natural selection result in better adapted individuals becoming more common in a population.
7. Species that don't adapt to a changing environment become **extinct**.

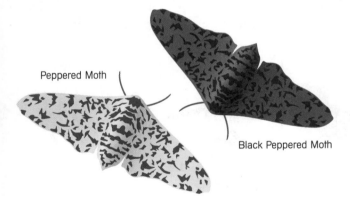

Peppered Moth

Black Peppered Moth

Natural selection led to a new variety of peppered moth. Peppered moths were originally pale and speckled, so they were camouflaged against the bark of silver birch trees, and **predators** (birds) couldn't see them very well.

During the industrial revolution, the air became polluted, and soot turned silver birch trees black. As a result, natural selection led to a new variety of peppered moth:

1. Dark peppered moths occurred as a result of a **genetic mutation** (i.e. mutants).
2. The dark moths competed with the pale moths.
3. The dark moths were **better adapted** to live in polluted areas as they were better camouflaged against the black bark.
4. The dark moths survived, reproduced and **passed on their genes**.
5. The number of dark moths in polluted areas increased.

When the Government passed the Clean Air Act, air pollution was reduced, and the bark on the trees stayed pale. The pale moth again had an advantage, so numbers began to grow.

Key Words

Evolution • Extinct • Fossil • Mutation • Organic • Reproduction

HT Evolution by Natural Selection

Charles Darwin (1809–1882) was a naturalist who put forward the theory of **evolution by natural selection**. The theory states that all organisms are in a struggle for survival and only the best-adapted survive. The survivors reproduce and pass on their well-adapted genes to their offspring. So gradually, a species will change.

Darwin had great difficulty in having his theory accepted, because…

- it's difficult to prove
- many scientists didn't accept it
- it contradicted the Bible – in those days, the Church had a massive influence over people's beliefs.

Environment

Classification

There are millions of different organisms and species. They are all classified according to their similarities and differences. There are five **kingdoms**:

- Plants
- Animals
- Fungi
- Protoctists
- Prokaryotes.

These kingdoms can then be divided into smaller, more specific groups. In the animal kingdom, for example, there are about 25 major groups called **phyla**.

- Phyla are then divided into smaller groups called **classes**.
- Classes are divided into **orders**.
- Orders are divided into **families**.
- Families are divided into **genera**.
- Each genus is split into individual **species**.

Usually a species will clearly fit into a group, but occasionally it isn't so obvious. For example, the duck-billed platypus has fur but it also has a bill and lays eggs, so which class does it belong to – mammals, birds or reptiles?

Vertebrates

All vertebrates belong to the same phylum and can be divided into five main classes:

Fish	Amphibians	Reptiles	Birds	Mammals
E.g. John Dory fish... • are cold-blooded • have gills • lay eggs in water • have scales.	E.g. frogs... • are cold-blooded • adults have lungs (young have gills) • lay eggs in water • have smooth skin.	E.g. snakes... • are cold-blooded • have lungs • lay eggs • have scaly skin.	E.g. skylarks... • are warm-blooded • have lungs • lay eggs • have feathers.	E.g. sheep... • are warm-blooded • have lungs • give birth to live offspring • have hair or fur on their skin.

Key Words

Classification

Glossary of Key Words

Adaptation – a change that improves an organism's ability to survive and reproduce in its environment.

Biomass – the total mass of organic material of an organism or population.

Characteristic – a feature of an organism.

Classification – the placing of all living organisms into groups, according to their characteristics.

Competition – occurs between species, or between members of the same species as a means of survival.

Ecosystem – all the plants and animals in a particular environment and the relationships between them and with their environment.

Environment – the area in which an organism lives or exists.

Evolution – the changes that take place in a species over a period of time, which result in the species being better adapted for survival.

Extinct – when a species dies out.

Food chain – the order in which energy and biomass are transferred from one organism to the next through feeding.

Fossil – the remains of an organism preserved in rock.

Genetic engineering – technology that involves transferring genes from one organism to another.

Genetically modified – an organism that has had new genes introduced into its genetic make-up.

Interdependence – where the population size of one species depends on the population size of another species.

Intra-species – between members of the same species.

Mutation – a spontaneous change in the genetic material of a cell.

Natural selection – the survival of individuals that are best adapted to their environment.

Organic (farming) – natural; of plant or animal origin.

Organism – a living thing.

Population – all the members of a species living in a defined area.

Predator – a creature that hunts and kills other creatures for food.

Prey – a creature that is hunted by other creatures.

Quantitatively – describes the amount of something.

Reproduction – the process of living organisms producing offspring.

Selective breeding – the process by which animals are selected and mated to produce offspring with desirable characteristics.

Species – a class of related living organisms that are able to breed and produce fertile offspring.

Practice Questions

1 What are the plants in a food chain called? Tick the correct option.

   A Herbivores ☐

   B Producers ☐

   C Carnivores ☐

   D Biomass ☐

2 Claire is studying the plants and animals that live in a stream. She draws this pyramid of their numbers:

Perch
Minnows
Water fleas
Microscopic algae

Which organism is the primary consumer? Tick the correct option.

   A Microscopic algae ☐

   B Water fleas ☐

   C Minnows ☐

   D Perch ☐

3 Which of the following do organisms **not** compete for in an ecosystem? Tick the correct option.

   A Space ☐

   B Food ☐

   C Water ☐

   D Warmth ☐

4 Kestrels (birds of prey) and mice have a predator–prey relationship. Tick the correct option to complete the following sentence. In a predator–prey relationship…

   A there are always more predators than prey ☐

   B there are always more prey than predators ☐

   C the numbers of predators and prey are always the same ☐

   D the numbers of predators and prey are always changing ☐

5 Explain the difference between natural selection and artificial selection.

_____

_____

_____

6 Choose the correct words from the options given to complete the following sentence.

milk   **cattle**   **poultry**   **increased**   **decreased**

Farmers selectively bred _____ so that the _____ yield was

_____.

7 Soya plants have been genetically engineered to make them herbicide-resistant. Number the following statements **1–4** to put them in the correct order.

A The gene is transferred to the embryo soya plant. ☐

B Genetically modified soya plants grow. ☐

C A herbicide-resistant weed is found. ☐

D The gene responsible for herbicide resistance is identified. ☐

8 Write **intensive** or **organic** next to each of the following statements to say whether the practice is carried out on intensive farms or organic farms.

a) Tend to specialise in one product, e.g. cattle or corn. _____

b) Use manual labour to get the work done. _____

c) Use lots of chemical fertilisers and pesticides. _____

d) Use manure. _____

9 Give two reasons why Charles Darwin had difficulty getting his theory of evolution by natural selection accepted.

a) _____   **b)** _____

10 For each of the five classes of vertebrates, list two features that help us to classify them.

a) Fish: **i)** _____   **ii)** _____

b) Amphibians: **i)** _____   **ii)** _____

c) Reptiles: **i)** _____   **ii)** _____

d) Birds: **i)** _____   **ii)** _____

e) Mammals: **i)** _____   **ii)** _____

Genes

Chromosomes, Genes and DNA

There are **two sets** of **chromosomes** in the **nucleus** of a human body **cell**:

- one set comes from the mother
- one set comes from the father.

There are 23 chromosomes in each set, so every cell has **46 chromosomes** in total (i.e. **23 pairs**).

Chromosomes are made up of **genes**. Genes…

- control how your cells function
- determine what **characteristics** you have.

Genes are made up of **DNA**. A DNA molecule consists of two coiled strands: a **double helix**.

Chemicals called **bases** stick out from each strand of a DNA molecule. They join so that the DNA molecule looks like a twisted ladder.

There are four bases: **adenine** (A), **cytosine** (C), **guanine** (G) and **thymine** (T).

- Adenine always links with thymine.
- Cytosine always links with guanine.

A cell

A section of chromosome

A section of a double helix

DNA double helix (a gene)

The Human Genome Project

The **Human Genome Project** (HGP) identified the sequence of bases in every human gene. There are 30 000 genes, so that meant identifying millions of base pairs.

There are concerns over who has access to the information, and how it could be misused.

But, knowing exactly where a gene appears on a chromosome, and how it's made up, could be very useful. For example…

- doctors could replace 'faulty' genes
- **forensic** scientists could use the information to compare DNA found at a crime scene with DNA from suspects.

HT Transgenic Animals

A transgenic animal is one that has had genes from another species added to its **genome**. It's been **genetically modified**.

Transgenic animals could be 'designed' to produce things that humans need for health and development.

For example, transgenic cows can produce 'designer milk', which contains…

- extra protein (casein)
- low levels of cholesterol
- human antibodies.

Gene Therapy

Gene therapy treats diseases and disorders by modifying a person's **genome**.

It's impossible to change the genes in every cell. But, by targeting specific areas, it's possible to achieve some degree of cure.

Viruses are used as vectors to deliver genetic material to the target cells. (The viruses are modified so they can't cause disease.)

Key Words

Antibodies • Cancer • Cell • Characteristic • Chromosome • DNA • Cystic fibrosis • Forensic • Gene • Gene therapy • Human Genome Project • Nucleus • Transgenic

HT Treating Cystic Fibrosis Genetically

Cystic fibrosis…

- affects cell membranes
- is caused by a recessive gene (i.e. it must be inherited from both parents).

People with cystic fibrosis…
- suffer from chest infections
- often have clogged airways
- can't digest food properly
- have a shorter life expectancy (40–50 years).

There's no cure for cystic fibrosis. But the symptoms can be treated, for example, by enzyme tablets, antibiotics or by using a bronchodilator to open the airways before chest physiotherapy. It could also be treated by gene therapy:

1. The patient is anaesthetised.
2. Whilst asleep they inhale the vector virus carrying the 'normal genes' through an aerosol.
3. Some of these 'normal genes' enter lung cells.
4. Patients feel much better for about four weeks.

A bronchodilator being used to open the airways

Treating Breast Cancer Genetically

Gene therapy also has the potential to be used for treating breast cancer.

Scientists have identified specific genes that, if present, increase the chance of a woman developing breast cancer.

Removing these problem genes and replacing them with normal, healthy genes would remove the risk. But, the genes would need to be removed from every cell. This could only be done by identifying and replacing the genes before they can multiply, i.e. as a fertilised egg.

Genes

Sexual Reproduction

During **fertilisation**, **gametes** (**haploid** cells, i.e. a sperm cell from the father and an egg cell from the mother) fuse together to produce a fertilised egg (**diploid** cell). So, the offspring gets…

- half its genes from its father
- half its genes from its mother.

This means that the offspring **inherit characteristics** from both parents. So, **sexual reproduction** leads to **variation** (differences). Each individual has a unique **genotype** (genetic make-up) The expression of these genes is called the **phenotype**.

Sexual reproduction ⮕ **Variation**

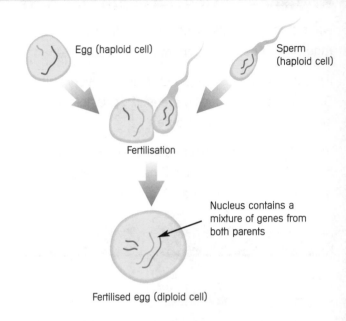

Egg (haploid cell)

Sperm (haploid cell)

Fertilisation

Nucleus contains a mixture of genes from both parents

Fertilised egg (diploid cell)

Asexual Reproduction

The offspring produced by **asexual reproduction** inherit their genes from only one parent. So, the offspring have exactly the same genes as the parent – they're genetically identical. This means that they don't show variation; they are **clones**.

Many plants naturally reproduce asexually, i.e. without flowers or fertilisation. For example, the *Chlorophytum* (spider plant) throws off **runners**:

1. The parent plant passes its genes on to its offspring.
2. The new individual is established.
3. The offspring has the same genes as the parent.

Asexual reproduction ⮕ **No variation**

Key Words

Asexual reproduction • Clone • Diploid • Environment • Fertilisation • Gamete • Generation • Genetics • Genotype • Haploid • Inheritance • Phenotype • Sexual reproduction • Transplant • Variation

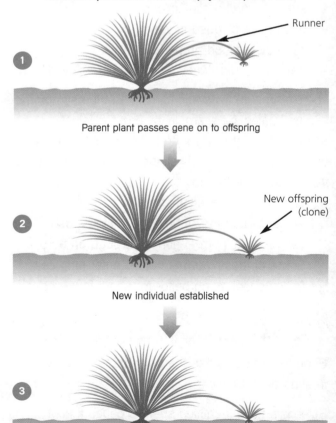

Asexual Reproduction of a Chlorophytum (Spider Plant)

Runner

1

Parent plant passes gene on to offspring

2

New offspring (clone)

New individual established

3

Offspring has the same genes as the parent plant

Clones

Clones are individuals that are **genetically identical**.

For example, identical twins and triplets are natural clones because they have the same genes.

It's possible to **produce clones artificially**. In 1996, Dolly the sheep became the first cloned mammal. Since then, lots of mammals have been produced using cloning techniques.

It's also possible to clone human body tissues and organs for **transplant surgery**.

But, some scientists, as well as the general public, have social and ethical concerns with cloning. These concerns include…

- the fear of creating the 'perfect race'
- the possibility of abnormalities occurring in clones
- clones will not have 'parents'.
- cloning doesn't allow 'natural' **evolution**.

Other people think that cloning is an inevitable result of scientific progress, and that we should be allowed to benefit from it.

HT 'Designer Babies'

Doctors and parents are now able to test embryos for genetic disorders and diseases, meaning healthy embryos can be selected. But, this has led to worries that, in future, people will select embryos on the basis of sex, cosmetic features, etc., resulting in a generation of **designer babies**'.

Many people feel that this goes against nature, or against 'God's will', so doctors and scientists are finding it difficult to have such scientific advances accepted.

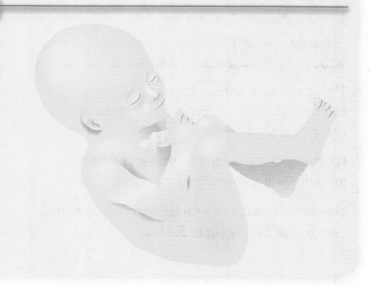

Variation

Variation is due to two factors:
- **Genetics (inheritance)** – variation due to the genes the individual inherits from their parents, for example, eye colour, natural hair colour.
- **Environment** – variation due to the conditions and surroundings in which an individual develops, for example, scars, languages spoken.

Genes

Variation: Inheritance and Environment

There has been a long debate over the relative importance of **inheritance** (genetic factors) and the **environment** (environmental factors) in determining certain **characteristics**.

It's now generally agreed that **variation** is due to a combination of genetic causes and environmental causes. The table illustrates this.

Feature	Genetic Factors	Environmental Factors
Sporting ability	• Natural ability and co-ordination • Natural physique and body structure	• Good coaching • Positive support • Good facilities and opportunities to practise
Intelligence	• The structure of the brain and its nerve connections	• Support from home • Quality of education • Life experience

Variation in Human Growth

The size of an organism is determined by a combination of genes. But, environmental factors can also affect it.

For example, a pregnant woman's diet will affect the birth weight of her baby.

The graph shows that women who take in more energy give birth to larger babies.

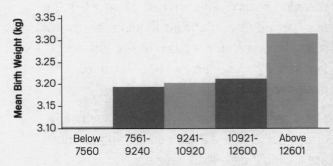

Variation in Plant Growth

The genes that plants inherit give them their potential to grow properly. But, in order to grow to their full potential, plants need minerals from the soil, which they absorb through their roots.

If the environment lacks the minerals the plants need, they can't grow properly, even with the right genes. For example...

- lack of phosphates results in poor root growth and small leaves
- lack of potassium results in yellowish leaves with dead patches.

Lack of phosphates   Lack of potassium

Alleles

Genes are the parts of chromosomes that control characteristics. There can be different versions for each gene. These are **alleles**. For example…

- the gene that controls tongue rolling has two alleles: one for being able to roll the tongue and one for being unable to roll the tongue
- the gene that controls earlobe type has two alleles: one for attached earlobes and one for unattached (free) earlobes.

Normal body cells contain pairs of chromosomes.

This means that genes also exist in pairs – one on each chromosome. So, for each gene, you'll have two matching alleles **or** two different alleles.

A **dominant** **allele** controls the development of a characteristic even if it's only present on one chromosome in a pair. A **recessive** **allele** controls the development of a characteristic only if it's present on **both** chromosomes in a pair.

Dominant and recessive forms of a gene lead to variation in a characteristic.

Inherited Diseases

Inherited diseases, like haemophilia, sickle cell anaemia and Huntington's disease are caused by 'faulty' alleles that come from one or both parents.

Haemophilia is caused by a recessive gene found on the X chromosome (a sex chromosome). It is sex linked. Because human males only have one X chromosome, this means that they only need one haemophilia gene to suffer from the condition.

Sickle cell anaemia occurs when a person inherits a 'faulty' recessive gene from each parent. Individuals who have only one faulty allele will not

have the disease but they are **carriers** so the faulty allele could be passed on to their offspring.

Huntington's disease is caused by a dominant allele: an individual only needs to inherit one faulty allele to have the disease.

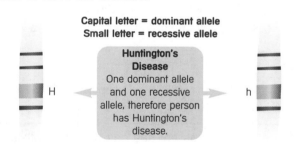

Capital letter = dominant allele
Small letter = recessive allele

Huntington's Disease
One dominant allele and one recessive allele, therefore person has Huntington's disease.

Genetic Variation

For each pair of genes, there are three possible combinations that produce different outcomes:

- When both alleles are dominant, the individual is **homozygous** **dominant** for that gene or condition.
- When both alleles are recessive, the individual is **homozygous recessive** for that gene or condition.
- When there's one dominant allele and one recessive allele, the individual is **heterozygous** for that gene or condition.

	Homozygous Dominant	Heterozygous	Homozygous Recessive
Earlobes	EE (free lobes)	Ee (free lobes)	ee (attached lobes)
Tongue rolling	TT (can roll)	Tt (can roll)	tt (can't roll)

Key Words

Allele • Carrier • Dominant • Heterozygous • Homozygous • Recessive

Genes

Monohybrid Inheritance

Simple genetic crosses can be performed to investigate **inheritance**. These simple crosses show **monohybrid inheritance** (i.e. the inheritance of a single gene).

You can use a grid or diagram to show these crosses.
- Capital letters represent dominant alleles.
- Lower case letters represent recessive alleles.

The possible outcomes for one pair of alleles are limited. But, there are numerous genes on the chromosomes in human body cells.

So, a lot of different combinations are possible, which is why individuals of the same species (even close relatives like brothers and sisters) show variation.

Examples of Monohybrid Inheritance

1 When one parent has two dominant genes, each offspring will inherit the dominant feature (each has a 100% chance of inheriting it).	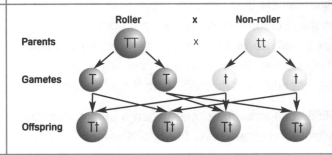
2 This can also be shown as a diagram. One parent has two dominant genes so each offspring will inherit the dominant feature.	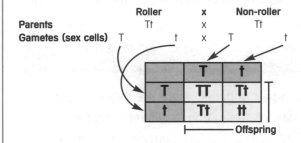
3 When each parent has one dominant allele and one recessive allele, each offspring has a 75% (3 in 4) chance of inheriting the dominant feature.	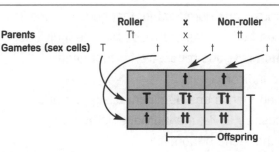
4 When one parent has one recessive allele and the other parent has two recessive alleles, each offspring has a 50% (1 in 2) chance of inheriting the dominant feature.	

Glossary of Key Words

Allele – an alternative form of a gene.

Asexual reproduction – a form of reproduction that doesn't involve fertilisation. The offspring are clones (i.e. genetically identical to the parent).

Carrier – an individual who carries a 'faulty' allele, but doesn't suffer from the condition caused by the faulty allele.

Cell – a basic unit of life.

Characteristic – a feature that an individual has.

Chromosome – made up of DNA and protein; consists of a series of genes.

Clone – an individual that is genetically identical to its parent.

Diploid – a cell that contains two copies (pairs) of each chromosome.

DNA (deoxyribonucleic acid) – the substance from which chromosomes are made.

Dominant – the stronger allele in a pair.

Environment – the area in which an organism lives or exists.

Fertilisation – the joining together of an egg with a sperm during sexual reproduction.

Forensic – the use of science in solving crimes, e.g. genetic fingerprinting, DNA testing.

Gametes – sex cells (i.e. sperm and eggs / ova).

Gene – the part of a chromosome that controls the development of characteristics individually or in combination with other, associated genes.

Gene therapy – the insertion of genes into a patient's cells and tissues to treat a disease or disorder.

Genetics – the study of how features are inherited.

Genotype – an individual's genetic identity.

Haploid – a cell that contains just one copy of chromosomes.

Heterozygous – different alleles in a genetic pair.

Homozygous – the same alleles in a genetic pair.

Human Genome Project (HGP) – an international project that set out to establish the sequence of all the bases in the genes of all 23 pairs of human chromosomes.

Inheritance – the passing on of features through reproduction.

Nucleus – the part of a cell that contains the chromosomes.

Phenotype – the physical expression of the genes that an individual possesses.

Recessive – the weaker allele in a pair.

Sexual reproduction – a form of reproduction that involves the fusion of an egg with a sperm during fertilisation.

Transplant – the transfer of an organ from one person to another.

Variation – the differences between organisms of the same species.

(HT) **Antibodies** – proteins made by white blood cells that neutralise antigens (i.e. chemicals made by microorganisms that enter the body).

Cancer – a disease that causes cells to divide uncontrollably to form tumours.

Cystic fibrosis – a disease that affects the cell membranes; inherited as the result of two recessive genes.

Generation – a group of individuals that represents a single stage in descent, e.g. grandfather, father and son are three generations.

Transgenic – an organism whose genome has received a gene / genes from another organism.

Practice Questions

1. Which of the following statements about DNA is correct? Tick the correct option.

    A Adenine always links with guanine ◯

    B Thymine always links with cytosine ◯

    C Cytosine always links with guanine ◯

    D Guanine always links with thymine ◯

2. The Human Genome Project has identified the base sequence for every human gene. Give two ways in which this information is useful to us.

    a) ....   b) ....

HT

3. Cystic fibrosis is an inherited disease for which there is no cure. However, its symptoms can be treated by gene therapy. Number the following statements **1–4** to put them into the correct order.

    A Some 'normal' genes enter the lungs. ◯

    B Patient inhales vector virus carrying 'normal' genes. ◯

    C Patient feels better. ◯

    D Patient is anaesthetised. ◯

4. a) Choose the correct words from the options given to complete the sentences below.

    genotype   characteristics   genes   parents   phenotype   variation

    Offspring inherit .... from both .... This leads to

    .... Each individual has a unique .... The expression of

    .... is called the ....

    b) Which type of reproduction does this paragraph refer to?

    ....

5. Explain why the offspring produced by asexual reproduction are clones.

    ....

HT

6. What is meant by the term 'designer babies'?

7 What two factors is variation due to?

a) ....   **b)** ....

8 Explain the difference between…

a) genes and alleles:

....

....

b) dominant and recessive:

....

....

9 Which of the following conditions are inherited? Tick the correct options.

A Haemophilia   ◯

B TB   ◯

C Sickle cell anaemia   ◯

D Cystic fibrosis   ◯

E Flu   ◯

F Huntington's disease   ◯

10 a) Explain the difference between the terms 'homozygous' and 'heterozygous'.

....

....

b) In humans, tongue rolling is a dominant feature.

Complete this diagram to show how parents who can both roll their tongue may have a child who can't roll their tongue. Explain the meaning of the symbols you have used.

....

Electrical & Chemical Signals

The Nervous System

The brain and the **spinal cord** make up the **central nervous system** (CNS). All the other **nerves** in the body are collectively known as the **peripheral nervous system**.

The nervous system allows you to react to your surroundings and coordinate your behaviour.

Humans have five **senses**. **Receptors** in the **sense organs** detect internal and external **stimuli** and allow the body to respond: sight (eyes), hearing (ears), taste (taste buds on the tongue), smell (chemical receptors in the nose), touch (receptors in skin). Balance can also be thought of as a sense (the receptors are the ears).

The receptors pass information along neurones to the **brain**. The brain coordinates the response:

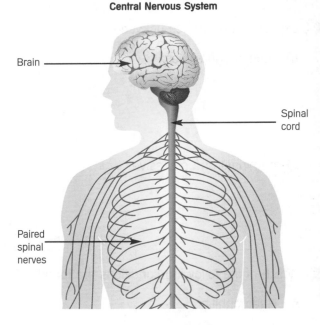

Central Nervous System

Brain

Spinal cord

Paired spinal nerves

Receptors	Sensory Neurones	Relay Neurones	Spinal Cord	Brain	Motor Neurones	Effectors

The Central Nervous System (CNS)

The Brain

The brain coordinates most of the body's actions:

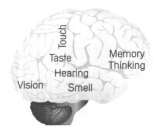

Touch
Taste
Hearing
Vision
Smell
Memory
Thinking

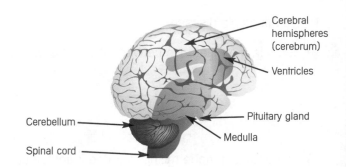

Cerebral hemispheres (cerebrum)

Ventricles

Cerebellum

Spinal cord

Pituitary gland

Medulla

HT Disruption to the Brain

The functioning of the brain may be disrupted:

- A tumour develops when brain cells grow uncontrollably. It presses on other parts of the brain, stopping them from working properly.
- A stroke occurs when part of the brain is starved of oxygen. If the affected part coordinates speech, the sufferer might not be able to speak properly after the stroke.

- Parkinson's disease develops when the brain stops producing **dopamine**, which allows brain cells to communicate. Lack of dopamine means the brain can't coordinate some things.
- *Grand mal epilepsy* is caused by random uncoordinated electrical signals between brain **neurones,** which cause epileptic fits.

Electrical & Chemical Signals

Neurones

Neurones are cells that carry **electrical impulses**. Neurones...

- are elongated (stretched out) to make connections between parts of the body
- have branched endings to allow one neurone to act on many muscle fibres or connect with many neurones.

① **Sensory neurones** take impulses from the receptors to the CNS.

② **Relay neurones** pass impulses from sensory neurones to motor neurones in the CNS.

③ **Motor neurones** take impulses from the CNS to the **muscles** or **glands**.

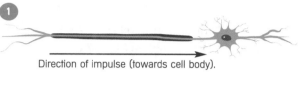

Direction of impulse (towards cell body).

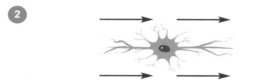

Impulse travels first towards, and then away from, cell body.

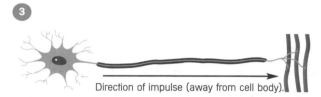

Direction of impulse (away from cell body).

The Synapse

When neurones pass information in and out of the CNS, they don't touch each other. There's a gap between them called the **synapse**.

① When an impulse reaches the synapse through the first neurone, a chemical transmitter is released, which diffuses across the synapse.

② This activates receptors on the second neurone.

③ An impulse is generated in the second neurone.

④ The chemical transmitter is destroyed.

A Synapse

Chemical transmitter released here

Impulse

Neurone A

Receptor area

Cell body of neurone B

Electrical impulse generated in neurone B

Measuring Reaction Times

Everyone needs to have fast reactions. Sometimes, you need very fast reactions.

You can measure your **reaction time** by catching a falling ruler.

If you catch it near the bottom, you have very quick reactions. If most of the ruler falls before you catch it, you have slower reactions.

Key Words

Brain • Central nervous system • Effector • Electrical impulse • *Grand mal* epilepsy • Motor neurone • Muscle • Nerve • Parkinson's disease • Peripheral nervous system • Reaction time • Receptor • Relay neurone • Sense organ • Sensory neurone • Stimulus • Stroke • Tumour

Electrical & Chemical Signals

Voluntary and Reflex Response

Voluntary **responses** are responses over which you have complete control. You consciously decide to do something. For example, speaking, picking something up.

Reflex **responses** are responses over which you have no control. Reflex responses happen automatically. For example, blinking, moving part of your body to avoid pain. Reflexes often protect you in some way.

Stimulus	Receptors	Coordinator	Effectors	Response
Freshly baked cake	Sight and smell receptors (i.e. eyes and nose)	**Sensory Neurones** ▼ **CNS** ▼ **Motor Neurones** ▶	Muscles in hand	Move hand to pick up cake

Stimulus	Receptors	Coordinator	Effectors	Response
Drawing pin	Pain receptor in finger (i.e. in the skin)	**Sensory Neurones** ▼ **Relay Neurone in Spinal Cord** ▼ **Motor Neurones** ▶	Muscles in hand	Withdraw hand

Example of a Reflex Response

When conscious action would be too slow to prevent harm to your body, reflex actions take place. Many reflex actions speed up response time by **missing out the brain**. The spinal cord alone acts as the coordinator. For example, if you put your hand on a drawing pin by accident, the **reflex arc** would follow this sequence:

1. The **receptors** in your skin are stimulated by the drawing pin (the stimulus).
2. **Impulses** pass along a **sensory neurone** into the spinal cord.
3. The sensory neurone **synapses** with a relay neurone.
4. The **relay neurone** synapses with a motor neurone, bypassing the brain.
5. Impulses pass along the **motor neurone** to the **muscles** (**effectors**), which contract and pull your hand away from the drawing pin.

The brain does receive nerve impulses about you pulling your hand away but only a split second after it has happened.

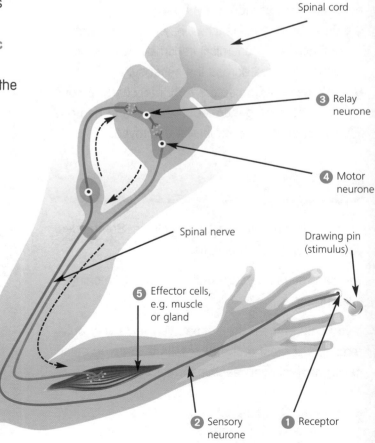

Spinal cord

❸ Relay neurone

❹ Motor neurone

Spinal nerve

Drawing pin (stimulus)

❺ Effector cells, e.g. muscle or gland

❷ Sensory neurone

❶ Receptor

Electrical & Chemical Signals

A Reflex Response – Accommodation

The **eye** is a **sense organ** that responds to light and focuses it onto receptor cells in the **retina**. This causes impulses to pass along sensory neurones to the brain. The **cornea** and the **lens** bend rays of light to form a clear image on the retina. This is called **focusing**.

Focusing on objects at different distances requires adjustments. This is called **accommodation**.

To focus on a **distant object**…
1. the ciliary body relaxes
2. the suspensory ligaments are pulled tight
3. the lens is pulled thinner and light isn't bent much.

To focus on a **near object**…
1. the ciliary body contracts
2. the suspensory ligaments become slack
3. the lens gets fatter and light is bent more.

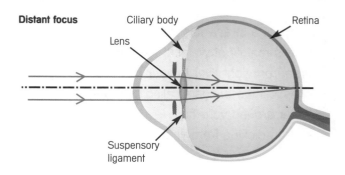

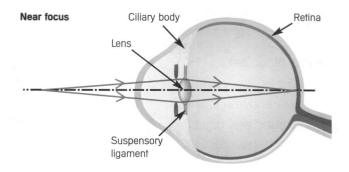

A Reflex Response – Iris Reflex

The **pupil** of the human eye increases and decreases in size in order to control the amount of light entering the eye. This is the **iris reflex**.

In dim light…
1. the radial muscles contract
2. the circular muscles relax
3. the pupil increases in size to let more light in.

In bright light…
1. the radial muscles relax
2. the circular muscles contract
3. the pupil decreases in size to reduce the amount of light let in.

Light on retina → Impulses along sensory neurones to brain → impulses from brain along motor neurones to iris → Pupil changes size

Dim light
Circular muscles relax
Radial muscles contract

Bright light
Circular muscles contract
Radial muscles relax

A Reflex Response – 'Ducking'

If you were walking along the road and suddenly a bird swooped low over your head, you would 'duck'. 'Ducking' is an automatic response to protect your head from harm.

Key Words
Iris reflex • Reflex • Reflex arc • Voluntary

Electrical & Chemical Signals

The Four Components of Blood

Plasma is a straw-coloured liquid that consists mainly of water. It transports…
- urea from your liver to your kidneys
- chemical messengers called **hormones**
- water around your body
- carbon dioxide from your organs to your lungs
- **glucose** and amino acids from your small intestine.

Platelets…
- help to clot the blood when you cut yourself.

Red blood cells…
- have no nucleus so they can be packed with **haemoglobin**
- pick up oxygen in your lungs, which combines with haemoglobin to form **oxyhaemoglobin**
- transport oxygen around your body
- are bi-concave in shape so they have a large surface area to absorb oxygen.

White blood cells…
- make antibodies to kill bacteria (lymphocytes)
- surround and digest bacteria (phagocytes).

Hormones and Coordination

Hormones coordinate and control how many parts of the body work. Hormones are produced by **endocrine glands** and are transported to their target organs through the bloodstream. For example, the pituitary gland produces **follicle-stimulating hormone** (FSH) and **luteinising hormone** (LH).

The Menstrual Cycle

Between the ages of roughly 13 and 50, the lining of a woman's uterus is replaced each month, so that she's ready to carry a baby. This is called the **menstrual cycle**.

HT

1. The uterus lining breaks down.
2. Oestrogen causes the uterus lining to thicken.
3. An egg is released by the ovary (this is ovulation).
4. Progesterone makes the lining stay thick, waiting for a fertilised egg.
5. If there's no fertilised egg, the uterus lining breaks down again and the cycle restarts.

Ovary

Follicle with egg gradually develops | Ovulation (egg released) | Empty follicle gradually disappears

Concⁿ of Hormone in the Blood

Progesterone

Oestrogen

Thickness of Wall

Uterus wall rich in blood vessels

0   7   14   21   28   7

Day of cycle

Natural Control of Fertility

The hormones **oestrogen** and **progesterone** control a woman's fertility:

- Oestrogen causes the lining of the uterus to thicken in preparation for carrying a baby.
- Progesterone preserves and maintains the uterus lining during the menstrual cycle.

If a woman becomes **pregnant**, her ovaries continue to produce progesterone, maintaining her uterus lining and preventing further ovulation.

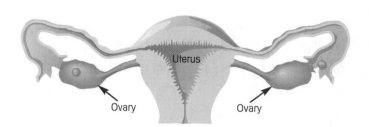

Artificial Control of Fertility

Oestrogen and progesterone can be artificially manufactured to control fertility.

Treating female infertility – if a woman naturally lacks oestrogen, she may not ovulate. Tablets containing synthetic oestrogen raise the body's oestrogen levels, therefore, triggering ovulation.

Contraception – the contraceptive pill contains oestrogen and progesterone. This prevents ovulation. The mini-pill contains only progesterone so ovulation occurs, but the cervix produces thick mucus to prevent the sperm getting to the eggs.

In-vitro Fertilisation

In-vitro **fertilisation** (IVF) can help couples who can't have a baby naturally.

1. The doctor inserts a thin tube through a cut in the woman's abdomen, and removes some eggs.
2. The eggs are kept in a solution of food and oxygen.
3. Sperm from the father is mixed with the eggs.
4. The fertilised eggs develop into embryos (groups of 4–8 cells).
5. Three (typically) of these embryos are placed in the uterus.

But, some people disagree with IVF:

- Is it right to interfere with a natural process in such an unnatural way?
- Should 'spare' embryos be destroyed, given to other women, or used for scientific research?

IVF is an expensive procedure, and multiple embryos in the uterus increase the risk of miscarriage. IVF also means that, theoretically, older, post-menopausal women could have babies, and many people think this is an inappropriate use of medical resources (money).

Key Words

Contraception • Follicle-stimulating hormone • Glucose • Hormone • Infertility • *In-vitro* fertilisation • Luteinising hormone • Menstrual cycle • Oestrogen • Pregnancy • Progesterone • Target organ

Electrical & Chemical Signals

Diabetes

Your body needs **glucose** for **respiration**. It's transported around your body in **blood plasma**.

The concentration of glucose in your blood is controlled by the hormone **insulin**. When the **pancreas** doesn't produce enough insulin, it can lead to **diabetes**.

Sometimes, diabetes can be controlled by diet (by reducing intake of carbohydrates). But, often, people who have diabetes control their blood sugar level by **injecting insulin**. Before injecting, they have to test the amount of sugar in their blood.

- If they've eaten food containing a lot of sugar or carbohydrate, a bigger dose of insulin is needed to reduce the blood sugar level.
- If they're going to be exercising (and, therefore, using up a lot of sugar), a smaller dose of insulin is needed.

Control of Blood Glucose

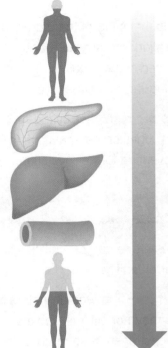

If the blood glucose concentration is too high…

… the pancreas releases insulin.

Glucose from the blood is then converted to insoluble glycogen in the liver…

… and is removed from the blood.

The blood glucose concentration returns to normal.

Producing Human Insulin

Human insulin can be produced by **genetic engineering**, using **genetically modified bacteria**:

1. The gene for insulin production is cut out of human DNA and inserted into bacterial DNA.
2. The bacterial DNA then reproduces.

This method of producing insulin means…
- it can be made more cheaply
- it can be made in large quantities.

Before human insulin was produced by genetic engineering, bovine (cow) insulin was used. But…
- it wasn't 100% effective
- there were side effects
- people were wary following the discovery that BSE could be passed to humans.

Some people are against genetic modification of organisms, but producing human insulin is an example where only good seems to have come of it.

Insulin gene 'cut out' of human DNA

Human insulin gene inserted into bacterial DNA

Bacterial DNA reproduce

Eventually large quantities are produced

Key Words

Bacteria • Diabetes • Genetically modified • Insulin • Pancreas

Electrical & Chemical Signals

Glossary of Key Words

Bacteria (singular: bacterium) – a single-celled microorganism that has no nucleus.

Brain – the organ in the body protected by the skull; part of the central nervous system.

Central nervous system (CNS) – the brain and the spinal cord.

Contraception – birth control, e.g. the pill, the condom.

Diabetes – a medical condition; the pancreas fails to produce enough insulin to control blood sugar.

Effector – the part of the body, e.g. a muscle or gland, that produces a response to a stimulus.

Electrical impulse – an electrical message that is passed along neurones when the nervous system communicates with parts of the body.

Follicle-stimulating hormone (FSH) – a hormone that causes an egg cell to mature in an ovary each month.

Genetically modified (GM) – an organism that's had DNA (a gene) transferred to it from another organism.

Glucose – a carbohydrate, or simple sugar; needed by humans for respiration.

Hormone – a chemical messenger produced by an endocrine gland.

Infertility – the inability to reproduce.

Insulin – the hormone produced by the pancreas that controls blood sugar levels in the body.

***In-vitro* fertilisation (IVF)** – a technique to fertilise an egg in artificial conditions, outside the female's body.

Iris reflex – the automatic opening and closing of the pupil in response to light conditions.

Luteinising hormone (LH) – a hormone that makes the ovary release an egg.

Menstrual cycle – the hormonally controlled changes that take place in a female's reproductive system; the monthly replacement of the uterus lining.

Motor neurone – a neurone that carries an impulse from the CNS to the muscles / glands.

Muscle – an organ made of cells that can change length to produce movement.

Nerve – a bundle of fibres running to tissues / organs in the body.

Oestrogen – a hormone produced by the ovaries; causes the uterus lining to thicken.

Pancreas – an organ in the abdomen that produces the hormone insulin.

Peripheral nervous system – all the nerves outside the brain and spinal cord.

Pregnancy – when a fertilised egg develops into an embryo inside a female's body.

Progesterone – a hormone produced by the ovaries; preserves and maintains the uterus lining during pregnancy.

Reaction time – how quickly a person responds to a stimulus.

Receptor – a sense organ that receives information from its environment.

Reflex – an automatic response to a stimulus; often to protect the body.

Reflex arc – the pathway of a reflex action.

Relay neurone – a neurone that carries an impulse from a sensory neurone to a motor neurone.

Sense organ – an organ in the body that detects a stimulus, i.e. the eyes, ears, tongue, nose and skin.

Sensory neurone – a neurone that carries an impulse from a receptor to the CNS.

Stimulus – a change in the environment that can be detected by a sense organ.

Target organ – an organ where a specific hormone will have an effect.

Voluntary – an action over which you have no conscious control.

HT ***Grand mal* epilepsy** – a form of epilepsy, a medical condition caused by spontaneous, uncoordinated electrical impulses in the brain.

Parkinson's disease – a disease of the brain that results in the gradual, progressive inability to move.

Stroke – caused by lack of oxygen to the brain; the brain stops working properly.

Tumour – a swelling that grows as a result of uncontrolled cell divisions; may be cancerous.

Practice Questions

1 Which statement correctly describes the central nervous system? Tick the correct option.

A The brain only ⬭

B The brain and the spinal cord ⬭

C The brain and the spinal nerves ⬭

D The spinal cord only ⬭

(HT)

2 Which of the following does **not** disrupt brain function? Tick the correct option.

A A tumour ⬭

B A stroke ⬭

C Parkinson's disease ⬭

D Huntington's disease ⬭

3 Draw lines between the boxes to match each term to its definition.

Sensory neurone	Takes nerve impulses from the CNS
Relay neurone	Passes impulses from one neurone to the next
Motor neurone	Passes impulses on in the CNS
Synapse	Takes impulses to the CNS

4 A synapse is a microscopic gap between two neurones. Number the following statements **1–4** to put them into the correct order to show what happens at the synapse.

A The chemical transmitter has been destroyed. ⬭

B The chemical transmitter diffuses across the synapse. ⬭

C The chemical transmitter is released by the first neurone. ⬭

D An electrical impulse is generated by the second neurone. ⬭

5 What is the difference between a voluntary response and a reflex response?

_____

_____

6 Reflex actions often protect your body in some way. Number the following statements **1–5** to describe how a reflex action works.

A Impulses pass along the sensory neurone. ⬜

B The relay neurone synapses with a motor neurone. ⬜

C Pain receptors in your skin are stimulated. ⬜

D The impulse passes to muscles. ⬜

E The sensory neurone synapses with the relay neurone. ⬜

7 Explain how your eye focuses on a distant object.

....

....

....

8 Your blood consists of four different components and each one does a different job. Complete this table by filling in the missing information.

Component of Blood	Function
Red blood cells	a) ....
b)	Make antibodies, digest bacteria
Platelets	c) ....
d)	Transport substances, e.g. urea, hormones, carbon dioxide, glucose and amino acids.

9 Explain how oestrogen and progesterone control a woman's fertility.

....

....

10 How does insulin lower blood sugar levels?

....

....

....

Use, Misuse & Abuse

Solvents

Solvents are depressants that give off different kinds of vapours. Solvents...

- can cause permanent damage to your lungs, liver, brain and kidneys if inhaled
- slow down reaction times by affecting neurones and slowing down transmission of a message across synapses
- cause hallucinations and change behaviour.

Alcohol

Alcohol is a depressant that contains the chemical ethanol. Alcohol...

- slows down reaction times by affecting neurones and slowing down transmission of a message across synapses
- can lead to depression and loss of self-control
- can lead to **brain damage** and **liver damage** (cirrhosis) if used long term
- can lead to unconsciousness, coma and death if used to excess.

Tobacco

Tobacco contains tar and nicotine, and produces carbon monoxide when it's smoked. Tobacco...

- can lead to **emphysema**, **bronchitis**, chest infections and **cancer** if used long term
- causes damage to the blood vessels, which can lead to circulatory system problems — heart attacks, strokes, and arterial and heart disease
- contains **nicotine**, which causes narrowing of the blood vessels, increases heart rate and blood pressure, and can lead to addiction
- gives off **carbon monoxide**, which is absorbed by haemoglobin more easily than oxygen.

The tar in cigarette smoke contains **carcinogens** (chemicals that cause cancer). These can cause cancer of the throat, lungs, mouth and stomach.

Emphysema is caused by excessive coughing. The alveoli get damaged, reducing the **surface area** for gaseous exchange. The person has to breathe more deeply, resulting in a barrel-shaped chest.

Key Words

Addiction • Alcohol • Bacteria •
Barbiturate • Caffeine • Cannabis •
Circulatory system • Depressant • Drug •
Gaseous exchange • Microbe •
Microorganism • Neurone • Opiate •
Overdose • Pain relief • Paracetamol •
Pathogen • Reaction time • Sedative •
Solvent • Stimulant • Synapse •
Tobacco• Transmission • Viral infection

Use, Misuse & Abuse

Drugs

Some **drugs** are obtained from plants; others are synthetic. Most drugs are used as medicines. Drugs alter how your body works. For example:

Caffeine and other **stimulants**…
- **speed up transmission** of nerve impulses along neurones and across synapses
- speed up your reactions
- can keep you awake.

Barbiturates and other **sedatives**…
- **slow down transmission** of nerve impulses along neurones and across synapses
- can make you **drowsy**, so you can't drive or do other activities that require concentration
- are addictive
- can make you feel angry, confused or upset.

Paracetamol and other **painkillers**…
- **prevent transmission** of nerve impulses along neurones and across synapses
- can make you **drowsy**, so you can't drive or do other activities that require concentration
- can have **side effects**, e.g. dizziness or itchiness.

Misuse of drugs can…
- cause physical and mental problems and alter the way you behave
- lead to other illnesses, e.g. sharing unsterilised needles when injecting illegal drugs can increase the risk of **viral infections** such as hepatitis and HIV
- cause death, e.g. **paracetamol** is a commonly used painkiller and anti-inflammatory. But, **overdosing** can lead to liver failure or death.

Cannabinoids and Opiates

Marijuana, **cannabis**, etc. (cannabinoids), and **opiates** are used for **pain relief**, especially in the terminally sick. But they're **addictive** and classed as illegal drugs so their use in helping patients is a controversial issue.

There's been a lot of scientific research into how effective cannabis is at controlling pain. Many doctors and scientists support the use of cannabis in controlled circumstances. Others feel more research is required.

Pathogens and Disease

Pathogens are disease-causing **microorganisms** (**microbes**). There are three main types of pathogen:

Bacteria	Fungi	Viruses
Bacteria, e.g. TB, conjunctivitis – treated by antibiotics.	**Fungi**, e.g. athlete's foot – treated by anti-fungal medicine and antibiotics.	**Viruses**, e.g. flu, chicken pox, HIV – very difficult to treat.

Use, Misuse & Abuse

Transmission of Microorganisms

Pathogens can be transmitted in two ways:

1 Direct contact –

- **Horizontal transmission**, e.g. touching an ill person.
- **Vehicle transmission**, e.g. touching an ill person's things.
- **Vertical transmission**, e.g. the disease is passed directly from mother to fetus across the placenta from the mother's blood to the unborn baby's blood. (HIV can be passed on in this way.)

2 Indirect contact –

- Many illnesses are spread through an infected person's **coughs / sneezes**, which release germs into the air.
- Some illnesses are spread by a third party **organism** – a **vector**. For example, if a mosquito bites a person who has malaria, then bites a healthy person, the mosquito transfers some of the ill person's blood to the healthy person, thereby passing on the illness. So, malaria is a **vector-borne** disease.

Physical and Chemical Barriers

Physical and chemical **barriers** are the body's first line of defence against microorganisms:

Skin – prevents entry of **disease**-causing microorganisms, prevents puncture, and prevents drying out and cracking because the **epidermis** is kept supple by oil from the sebaceous glands.

Blood clotting – **platelets** are tiny particles in the blood that help it to clot when a blood vessel is damaged at a cut. When exposed to air, platelets release an enzyme. This converts a soluble protein into insoluble protein called **fibrin**. The fibrin forms a mesh that traps red blood cells and a clot forms, which hardens to form a scab.

Cilia – tiny hairs found on specialised cells in the airways of the respiratory system. They beat the mucus (produced by other cells) towards the mouth. The mucus traps dust and microorganisms, which the cilia push out of the lungs to be swallowed.

Nasal hairs – trap dust and other particles and prevent them being breathed into the lungs.

Lysozyme – an enzyme that digests the cell walls of bacteria that land on the eye, thereby killing the bacteria.

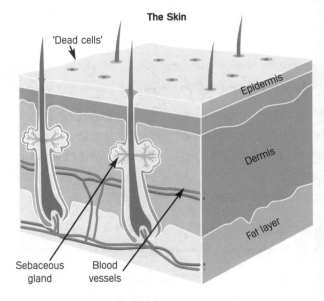

The Skin

'Dead cells'

Epidermis

Dermis

Fat layer

Sebaceous gland

Blood vessels

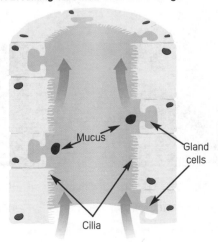

A Breathing Tube with Cilia in the Lungs

Mucus

Gland cells

Cilia

Non-specific Defence

The body's second line of defence against microorganisms is **non-specific defences**:

- inflammatory response
- **white blood cells** (phagocytes).

At the site of an infection, the blood vessels become enlarged. This increases blood flow to the area and makes the skin look red. The capillaries in the skin become more permeable so fluids leak out of the blood vessels into the tissues. This causes inflammation.

Where this has occurred, **white blood cells** called **phagocytes** change shape and move out of the blood through the capillary walls into the surrounding tissues. They ingest the microorganisms at the site of the infection and die, forming pus.

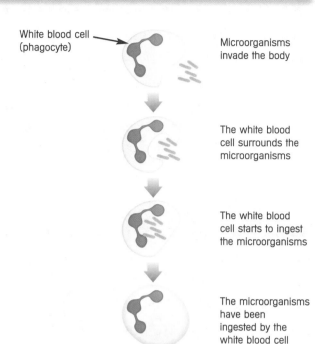

White blood cell (phagocyte)

Microorganisms invade the body

The white blood cell surrounds the microorganisms

The white blood cell starts to ingest the microorganisms

The microorganisms have been ingested by the white blood cell

Specific Defence

The body's third line of defence against microorganisms is **specific defence**:

- white blood cells
- the immune system.

White blood cells called **lymphocytes** recognise invading microorganisms as antigens or foreign bodies. They produce antibodies to destroy them. You feel ill because it takes time for the lymphocytes to produce antibodies. The antibodies are produced much more quickly if you've already had the infectious disease. The lymphocytes remember the antigen and can produce antibodies much faster, providing you with natural immunity.

Key Words

Antibodies • Antigen • Barrier • Cilia • Disease • Foreign body • Immune system • Infection • Inflammation • Lysozyme • Organism • Vector-borne • White blood cell

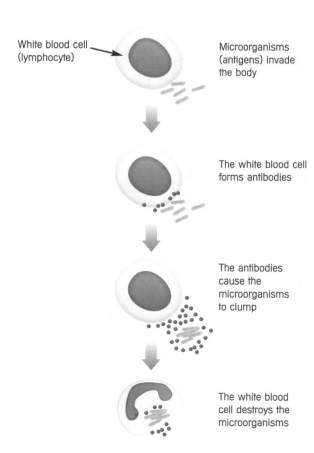

White blood cell (lymphocyte)

Microorganisms (antigens) invade the body

The white blood cell forms antibodies

The antibodies cause the microorganisms to clump

The white blood cell destroys the microorganisms

Use, Misuse & Abuse

Tuberculosis

Tuberculosis (TB) is a disease caused by the bacterium *Mycobacterium tuberculosis*.

TB is spread through indirect contact – infected people spread it when they cough and sneeze tiny particles containing the bacteria into the air. If a healthy person breathes the particles in, they're likely to become infected.

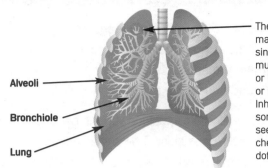

Alveoli

Bronchiole

Lung

The TB bacteria may cause single or multiple cavities or lumps in one or both lungs. Inhaled TB can sometimes be seen on a chest X-ray as dots of calcium

HT Tuberculosis in Britain

In Britain, TB tends to occur in inner cities: in 2001 London recorded 41% of all cases in England, Wales and Northern Ireland.

In an effort to **prevent** TB, in 1953 the **BCG vaccine** was given to school children aged about 13. But, because of the high costs, the policy was changed in 2005 and the vaccine's now only given to people considered to be 'at risk'. TB is controlled by **drug therapy**. Normal antibiotics don't kill TB bacteria, so a combination of three or four **anti-TB antibiotics** must be taken for six months to treat it. Some people are infected with 'multi-drug-resistant TB' and must take antibiotics for up to two years.

The graph shows how many people have had TB in Britain since 1913. It shows that...
- cases fell dramatically up to 1940
- cases fell gradually between 1950 and 1990
- there's recently been an increase in cases.

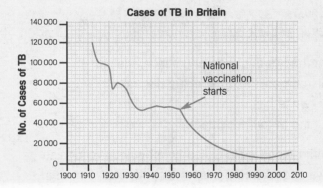

Cases of TB in Britain

National vaccination starts

Development of New Medicines

New **drugs** have to be thoroughly tested and trialled before they can be prescribed by doctors and given to patients. Trialling a drug has three stages:
1. Testing for **toxicity**.
2. Testing to see if it's **safe** for human use.
3. Testing to see if it **works**.

These three stages can take years to complete and cost hundreds of thousands of pounds.

1 Is it toxic?	Laboratory tests establish whether the drug is toxic. These tests are often carried out on lab animals, like rats.
2 Is it safe for humans?	Human volunteers trial the drug to see whether there are any side effects for humans.
3 Does it work?	People with the illness that the drug is supposed to cure are tested.

Key Words

Tuberculosis

Glossary of Key Words

Addiction – a dependency on something, e.g. a drug, tobacco, alcohol.

Alcohol – fermented liquid that has a sedative effect.

Antibodies – proteins that are made by white blood cells in order to destroy microorganisms (antigens) that invade the body.

Antigens – foreign bodies that enter the body.

Bacteria (singular: bacterium) – a single-celled microorganism that has no nucleus.

Barbiturate – a type of sedative.

Barrier – a surface that prevents things from passing through.

Caffeine – a type of stimulant.

Cannabis – an illegal drug obtained from the cannabis plant. (Part of the cannabinoids.) It is a hallucinogen.

Cilia – small, hair-like structures that are found on the surface of some cells, e.g. cells that line the trachea.

Circulatory system – consists of the blood, blood vessels (arteries, capillaries and veins) and heart.

Depressants – chemicals that slow down the transmission of a nerve impulse across a synapse.

Disease – an illness caused by a pathogen.

Drug – a chemical substance that alters the way the body works or responds.

Foreign body – something in the body that shouldn't be there, e.g. a microorganism, a wood splinter.

Gaseous exchange – the exchange of oxygen and carbon dioxide for respiration. Gaseous exchange happens in the lungs.

Immune system – the body's mechanism for defending itself against disease.

Infection – occurs when the body is invaded by microorganisms.

Inflammation – when part of the skin or body becomes swollen, red and sometimes painful. It's often the result of infection or injury.

Lysozyme – an enzyme that breaks down bacterial cell walls. It's found in tears and protects the eye from harmful bacteria.

Microbe – an organism that can only be seen with a microscope (same as microorgansim).

Microorganism – an organism that can only be seen with a microscope (same as microbe).

Neurone – a cell that carries nerve impulses.

Opiate – a drug obtained from opium.

Organism – a living thing.

Overdose – an excessive (usually dangerous and potentially fatal) dose of a drug.

Pain relief – stops the transmission of a message across a synapse, thereby, relieving pain. Some drugs / medicines can provide pain relief.

Paracetamol – a pain-relief medicine.

Pathogen – a microorganism that causes disease.

Reaction time – how quickly a person responds to a stimulus.

Sedative – a chemical that slows down the transmission of a message across a synapse.

Solvent – a substance that can dissolve other substances. Usually volatile and flammable, solvents are sometimes deliberately inhaled (solvent abuse).

Stimulant – a chemical that speeds up the transmission of a nerve impulse across a synapse.

Synapse – the small gap between neurones.

Tobacco – obtained from the dried leaves of the tobacco plant. It contains nicotine, which is addictive.

Transmission – the transfer of something from one thing to another (e.g. a disease from one person to another).

Tuberculosis – a bacterial infection that develops tubercles (lumps) in internal organs, often the lungs.

Vector-borne – a disease-causing microorganism that is transmitted by another organism (the vector).

Viral infection – an infection caused by a virus.

White blood cell – part of the body's immune system. Two important types are phagocytes and lymphocytes.

Practice Questions

1. Solvents are depressants. List three ways in which they affect your body.

   a) ....

   b) ....

   c) ....

2. Draw lines between the boxes to match each term to its correct definition.

Alcohol	A substance that alters how the body works
Caffeine	A drug obtained from opium
Drug	Pain relief medicine
Opiate	Fermented liquid that acts as a sedative
Paracetamol	A stimulant

3. List four ways in which smoking tobacco can damage your health.

   a) ....

   b) ....

   c) ....

   d) ....

4. Explain the difference between stimulants and sedatives.

   ....

   ....

5. Which of the following is **not** a microbe? Tick the correct option.

   A Bacteria

   B Fungi

   C Fleas

   D Viruses

6 Circle the correct options in the following sentences.

a) **Direct / Indirect** contact describes illnesses and diseases that are spread by touching an ill person or their things. The spread of disease by touching another person is known as **horizontal / vehicle / vertical** transmission. When a mother infects her fetus across the placenta, this is known as **horizontal / vehicle / vertical** transmission.

b) **Direct / Indirect** contact describes illnesses and diseases that are spread by coughs and sneezes, germs in the air that are breathed in, or through a third party.

7 Circle the correct options in the following sentences.

a) Skin prevents **microbes / fungi** from entering your body. It acts as **a barrier / an antibiotic**.

b) **Cilia / Platelets** are found in airways. They waft **mucus / lysozyme** out that traps dust and microbes.

c) Lysozyme is **an enzyme / an antibody** found in the eye, which kills bacteria by digesting their cell wall.

8 White blood cells (phagocytes) protect your body. Number these statements **1–4** to put them into the correct order and describe how phagocytes protect your body.

A Phagocytes surround bacteria. 〇

B Bacteria are digested. 〇

C Bacteria invade the body. 〇

D Phagocytes start to digest the bacteria. 〇

9 Describe how tuberculosis (TB) is spread.

....

....

....

10 What three things must new drugs / medicines be tested for?

a) ....

b) ....

c) ....

Patterns in Properties

Atoms

All chemical **elements** are made up of **atoms**. Atoms have…

- a small **nucleus** made up of **protons** and **neutrons**
- **electrons** surrounding the nucleus.

All atoms of the same element have the same number of protons and electrons in each of their atoms. This table shows the relative charges of the different particles.

Atomic Particle	Relative Charge
Proton	+1 (**positive**)
Neutron	0 (no charge)
Electron	-1 (**negative**)

An atom has the same number of protons as electrons, so the atom as a whole is **neutral** (i.e. it has no electrical charge).

The **atomic number** of an element is the number of protons (or electrons) in one atom.

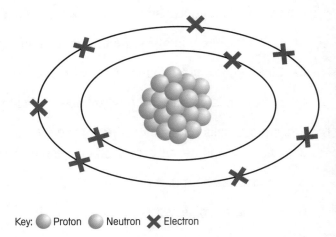

Key: ● Proton ● Neutron ✕ Electron

Molecules

Molecules are formed when two or more atoms are joined together. **Diatomic molecules** are made up of only two atoms, for example, the oxygen molecule has the **formula** O_2.

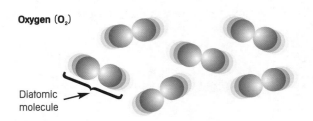

Oxygen (O_2)

Diatomic molecule

Compounds

Compounds are formed when **elements** are joined together in a chemical reaction. The compound's properties will be different to the properties of the elements it's made from.

For example, when iron and sulphur are heated, they form the compound iron(II) sulphide:

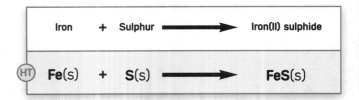

Iron + Sulphur ⟶ Iron(II) sulphide

(HT) $Fe(s)$ + $S(s)$ ⟶ $FeS(s)$

The compound iron(II) sulphide contains iron ions joined to sulphide ions. Compounds can only be split into simpler substances through chemical reactions.

Key Words

Atom • Atomic number • Compound • Diatomic molecules • Electron • Element • Endothermic • Exothermic • Formula • Molecule • Negative • Neutral • Neutron • Positive • Proton

Patterns in Properties

Chemical Reactions

A **chemical reaction** can involve two or more **reactants** combining together to make **products**.

Chemical reactions happen at **different rates** and are accompanied by a heat change. Reactions can be...
- **exothermic** – heat given out
- **endothermic** – heat taken in.

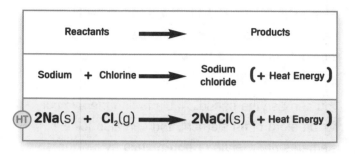

Reactants	→	Products
Sodium + Chlorine →		Sodium chloride (+ Heat Energy)
(HT) $2Na(s) + Cl_2(g)$ →		$2NaCl(s)$ (+ Heat Energy)

(HT) Balancing Equations

In all chemical reactions, the total mass of the **reactants** is equal to the total mass of the **products**. This means that there must be the same number of atoms on both sides of the equation.

Follow these steps to write a balanced equation:

1. Write a word equation for the reaction.
2. Write the correct formula for each of the reactants and the products.
3. Balance the equation by adding numbers in front of the reactants and / or products.
4. Write a balanced symbol equation

N.B. *Make sure you use the state symbols: (s) for solids, (l) for liquids, (g) for gases and (aq) for aqueous solutions.*

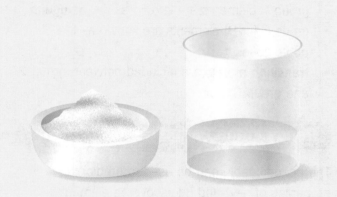

	Reactants	→	Products
1 Write a word equation	**Magnesium + Oxygen**	→	**Magnesium oxide**
2 Substitute in formulae	**Mg + O_2**	→	**MgO**
3 Balance the equation	Mg + O O	→	Mg O

- There are two oxygen atoms on the reactant side, but only one oxygen atom on the product side. We need to add another **MgO** to the product side to balance the oxygen atoms.
- We now need to add another **Mg** on the reactant side to balance the **Mg**s.
- There are two magnesium atoms and two oxygen atoms on each side – **it is balanced**.

4 Write a balanced symbol equation → **$2Mg(s) + O_2(g)$** → **$2MgO(s)$**

Patterns in Properties

The Periodic Table

Elements are arranged in the **periodic table** in order of increasing **atomic number**. A row of elements is called a **period**. A column of elements is called a **group**.

You can use the periodic table to find the **symbol** for an atom of an element. You can also tell if elements are **metals** or **non-metals** by looking at their position in the table.

In the periodic table...

- group 1 elements are known as the **alkali metals**
- group 7 elements are known as the **halogens**
- group 0 (or 8) elements are known as the **noble gases**
- **transition metals** are included between group 2 and group 3.

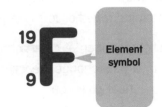

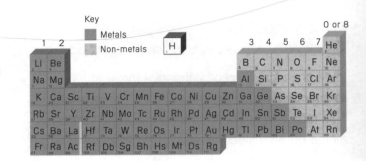

Trends in the Periodic Table

The periodic table can be used to predict the properties of new and undiscovered elements.

Elements that have **similar properties** are in the same group as they have the same number of electrons in the outer shell of their atoms.

The mass of the elements **increase** from left to right across a period.

Elements in group 1 become **more reactive** down the group. Elements in group 7 become **less reactive** down the group.

HT The History of the Periodic Table

Before the modern periodic table was developed, attempts were made to arrange the elements.

In 1817, **Johann Dobereiner** developed the 'law of triads'. Each triad was made up of three elements that had similar reactions and appearances.

In 1864, **John Newlands** proposed the 'Newlands' Law of Octaves'. Known elements were arranged in order of increasing relative atomic mass. Newlands found that every eighth element had similar properties but this didn't work for the heavier elements.

In 1869, **Dimitri Mendeleev** developed the modern periodic table. Elements were arranged in order of increasing relative atomic mass and in groups. He left gaps for undiscovered elements and was able to work out the atomic mass and properties of undiscovered elements.

In 1913, **Henry Moseley** proposed the use of **atomic number**, leading to the modern periodic table.

The Alkali Metals

The **alkali metals** are found in **group 1** of the periodic table.

Members of this group include…

* lithium
* sodium
* potassium.

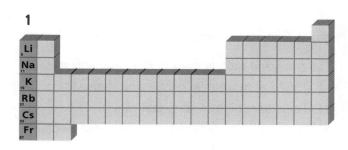

Properties of Alkali Metals

Alkali metals have similar properties:

* They are soft and have low melting points.
* They are very reactive and must be stored under oil.
* They react vigorously with water to form hydroxides and hydrogen gas.

The properties of alkali metals change with increasing **atomic number**. The further down group 1 the metal is…

* the **greater** its reactivity
* the **lower** its melting and boiling point.

Reactions of Alkali Metals

The reactivity of alkali metals with water increases down the group:

* Lithium reacts steadily.
* Potassium reacts so vigorously it melts and the hydrogen evolved catches fire.
* Caesium explodes, shattering the container.

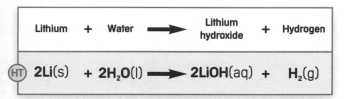

Lithium + Water ⟶ Lithium hydroxide + Hydrogen

(HT) $2Li(s) + 2H_2O(l) \longrightarrow 2LiOH(aq) + H_2(g)$

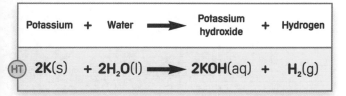

Potassium + Water ⟶ Potassium hydroxide + Hydrogen

(HT) $2K(s) + 2H_2O(l) \longrightarrow 2KOH(aq) + H_2(g)$

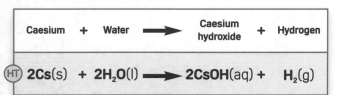

Caesium + Water ⟶ Caesium hydroxide + Hydrogen

(HT) $2Cs(s) + 2H_2O(l) \longrightarrow 2CsOH(aq) + H_2(g)$

Key Words

Alkali metal • Group • Halogen • Noble gases • Period • Symbol • Transition metals

Patterns in Properties

The Transition Metals

The **transition metals** are included between group 2 and group 3 of the periodic table, e.g. copper, nickel and iron.

The transition metals have similar properties:
- They are malleable, ductile and dense.
- They have high melting points.
- They are good conductors of heat and electricity.
- They are not very reactive.
- Their compounds are often coloured.

The transition metals are used to make wires, coins, girders, alloys and jewellery and their compounds are used as **catalysts**.

Reactions of the Transition Metals

Many transition metal ions form solids from **solution** when they are reacted with dilute sodium hydroxide. This **precipitation reaction** is used to help identify an unknown metal cation within a compound. For example:

Colour of Precipitate	Metal ions present		Solid dissolves in ammonia solution
Pale blue	Copper	Cu^{2+}	Yes
Green	Iron	Fe^{2+}	No
Red–brown	Iron	Fe^{3+}	No
White	Zinc	Zn^{2+}	Yes

Copper ions +	Sodium hydroxide	→	Copper hydroxide	+	Sodium ions

HT $Cu^{2+}(aq) + 2NaOH(aq) \rightarrow Cu(OH)_2(s) + 2Na^+(aq)$

The Noble Gases

The **noble gases** are found in group 0 (or group 8) of the periodic table. The noble gases are **chemically inert**, i.e. unreactive, compared to other elements in the periodic table.

They are used in the following way:
- Helium is used in airships and weather balloons because it's much less dense than air and is non-flammable.
- Argon is used in light bulbs because it's unreactive and provides an inert atmosphere.
- Argon, krypton and neon are all used in fluorescent lights and discharge tubes.

Key Words

Displacement reaction • Halide • Inert • Precipitation • Solution

Patterns in Properties

The Halogens

The **halogens** are found in **group 7** of the periodic table. There are five non-metals in group 7. All halogens exist as **diatomic molecules**.

The further down group 7 the element is…
- the **lower** its reactivity
- the **higher** its melting and boiling points.

Chlorine is used in water purification as it kills bacteria. It's also used for bleaching paper, wood and cloth. Iodine in solution is used as an antiseptic.

Halogen	Boiling Point (°C)	Colour / Physical State at Room Temperature
Fluorine	-188°C	Pale yellow vapour
Chlorine	-34°C	Pale green vapour
Bromine	59°C	Red–brown liquid
Iodine	187°C	Dark grey solid

Displacement Reactions

The further down the group a halogen is, the **less reactive** it is. This can be shown by the **displacement reactions** of halogens with solutions of other **halides**.

Chlorine is the most reactive and will displace both bromine and iodine, while bromine will displace iodine.

	Potassium Chloride	Potassium Bromide	Potassium Iodide
Chlorine Cl_2	✕	Potassium chloride	Potassium chloride
Bromine Br_2	No reaction	✕	Potassium bromide
Iodine I_2	No reaction	No reaction	✕

Reactions of Halogens and Iron

When iron (in the form of iron wool) is heated strongly with the halogens, the **same reaction** takes place but the reactivity **decreases** down the group:
- When iron reacts with **chlorine** gas, the iron wool glows bright red–orange.
- When iron reacts with **bromine** vapour, the iron wool glows orange.
- When iron reacts with **iodine** vapour, the iron wool only just glows orange.

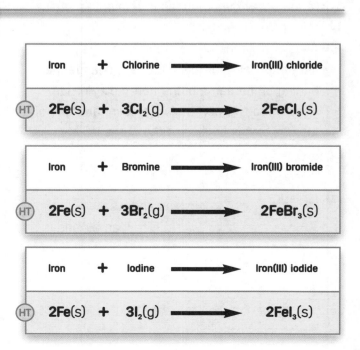

Iron + Chlorine ⟶ Iron(III) chloride

(HT) $2Fe(s) + 3Cl_2(g) \longrightarrow 2FeCl_3(s)$

Iron + Bromine ⟶ Iron(III) bromide

(HT) $2Fe(s) + 3Br_2(g) \longrightarrow 2FeBr_3(s)$

Iron + Iodine ⟶ Iron(III) iodide

(HT) $2Fe(s) + 3I_2(g) \longrightarrow 2FeI_3(s)$

Patterns in Properties

Metal Compounds and Flame Tests

Flame tests can be used to identify some metal cations within **compounds** because some metal **ions** produce distinctive **colours** when their chlorides are heated in a flame. Use this method:

1. Dip a piece of nichrome (nickel-chromium alloy) wire in concentrated hydrochloric acid to clean it, then dip it in the compound.
2. Heat deposit the wire in a Bunsen flame.

The table below shows the distinctive colours that are produced.

By understanding how different chemical substances behave and the tests used to identify them, scientists can use these **analytical** techniques to identify unknown substances. This can be very useful, for example, in forensic science.

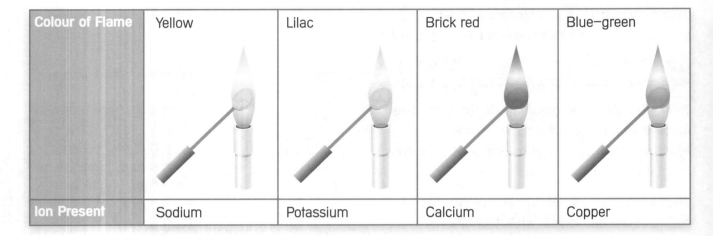

Colour of Flame	Yellow	Lilac	Brick red	Blue–green
Ion Present	Sodium	Potassium	Calcium	Copper

HT Naming Metal Compounds

There are a few general rules to remember when naming metal compounds:

- Always write the name of the metal first. If there is one non-metal present, change the ending of the name of the non-metal to **-ide**.
- If there are two non-metals present and one of them is oxygen, then end the name in **-ate**.

Examples

Sodium + Chlorine $\longrightarrow$ Sodium chloride
$2Na(s) + Cl_2(g) \longrightarrow 2NaCl(s)$

Copper + Sulphuric acid $\longrightarrow$ Copper sulphate + Hydrogen
$Cu(s) + H_2SO_4(aq) \longrightarrow CuSO_4(aq) + H_2(g)$

Key Words

Analytical • Flame test

Glossary of Key Words

Alkali metal – an element found in group 1 of the periodic table. Atoms of these elements all contain a single electron in their outer shell.

Analytical – a variety of methods used to identify the components of substances.

Atom – the smallest part of an element that can enter into a chemical reaction.

Atomic number – the number of protons in an atom.

Compound – a substance in which the atoms of two or more elements are chemically joined, either by ionic or covalent bonds.

Diatomic molecules – molecules that consist of two atoms; used in relation to elements that only exist at the smallest level as pairs of atoms (never as single atoms), e.g. oxygen (O_2).

Displacement reaction – a chemical reaction in which a more reactive element displaces a less reactive element in the compound.

Electron – a negatively charged subatomic particle that orbits the nucleus in an atom.

Element – a substance that consists of only one type of atom.

Endothermic – a chemical reaction that takes in heat from its surroundings so that the products have more energy than the reactants.

Exothermic – a chemical reaction that gives out energy (heat) to its surroundings so that the products have less energy than the reactants.

Flame test – a test to identify some metal ions in compounds from the colour of flame produced when their chlorides are placed in a Bunsen flame.

Formula – a written representation of the elements present in a chemical compound that shows the number of atoms of each element present.

Group – a vertical column of elements in the periodic table.

Halide – a compound of a halogen.

Halogen – an element found in group 7 of the periodic table.

Inert – a substance that is chemically unreactive.

Molecule – the smallest part of an element or compound that can exist on its own in the free state.

Negative – having a negative charge; lower than 0.

Neutral – having neither a positive nor a negative charge.

Neutron – a particle found in the nucleus of an atom that has no electrical charge.

Noble gases – unreactive, non-metallic elements found in group 0 (or 8) of the periodic table.

Positive – having a positive charge; higher than 0.

Period – a horizontal row of elements in the periodic table.

Precipitation – when an insoluble solid is formed from two solutions as a result of a chemical reaction.

Proton – a positively charged particle found in the nucleus of an atom.

Solution – the mixture formed when a solute dissolves in a solvent.

Symbol – equal to 1 mol of atoms.

Transition metals – most of the metal elements found in the central block of the periodic table.

Practice Questions

1 What three particles would you expect to find in an atom?

a) ....

b) ....

c) ....

2 The atomic number of an element tells you what about the element?

....

3 What is formed when two or more elements are joined together in chemical reactions? Tick the correct option.

A Atoms ▢   **B** Elements ▢

C Compounds ▢   **D** Reactants ▢

4 What type of chemical reaction will give out heat?

....

5 Which two elements combine to make the compound iron sulphide?

....

HT

6 Write down the balanced equation for the following reaction:
Copper oxide + Carbon ⟶ Copper + Carbon dioxide

....

7 Why was Mendeleev's table helpful in the development of the modern periodic table?

....

8 a) What compound is formed when you react magnesium with sulphuric acid?

....

b) What compound is formed when you react sodium with oxygen?

9 Using the periodic table, how can you tell if an element is a metal or a non-metal?

....

10 What is the common name for the group 1 metals? Tick the correct option.

    A Semi-precious metals ◯

    B Alkali metals ◯

    C Transition metals ◯

    D Alkaline earth metals ◯

11 What happens to the reactivity of elements in group 1 as the atomic number increases?

....

12 Many transition metals compounds in solution react with sodium hydroxide solution. What type of reaction is this?

....

13 Which of the following properties would you expect transition metals to have? Tick the correct options.

    A Malleable ◯   **B** Dense ◯

    C Low melting points ◯   **D** Good conductors of heat ◯

14 Why is helium used in airships and weather balloons?

....

15 Name the elements in group 7 of the periodic table.

....

16 Give two uses of chlorine.

a) ....

b) ....

17 Describe what happens when iron, in the form of iron wool, is heated strongly with iodine.

....

Making Changes

Metal Ores

Ores are naturally occurring rocks found in the Earth's crust. They contain compounds of metals that can be extracted. Some of these compounds are **metal oxides**.

The method of extracting a metal from its ore depends on its position in the **reactivity series**:

- The most reactive metals form the most stable ores and are the most difficult to extract. Electroysis is used.
- The least reactive metals are found uncombined in the Earth's crust and are the easiest to extract from their ores.

Reactivity Series

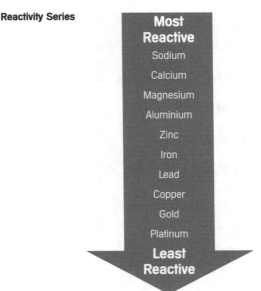

Reduction

Reduction can be the **loss of oxygen** from a compound during a chemical reaction. The metal compound is broken down to give the metal element.

For example, when copper oxide and lead oxide are heated with carbon, the carbon is oxidised to produce carbon dioxide and the copper oxide and lead oxide are reduced to the metal.

| Copper oxide | + | Carbon | Heat → | Copper | + | Carbon dioxide |

(HT) $2CuO(s) + C(s) \xrightarrow{Heat} 2Cu(s) + CO_2(g)$

| Lead oxide | + | Carbon | Heat → | Lead | + | Carbon dioxide |

(HT) $2PbO(s) + C(s) \xrightarrow{Heat} 2Pb(s) + CO_2(g)$

Oxidation

Oxidation can be the **gaining of oxygen** by an element or compound. For example, when magnesium is heated with oxygen it's oxidised to produce magnesium oxide.

| Magnesium | + | Oxygen | Heat → | Magnesium oxide |

(HT) $2Mg(s) + O_2(g) \xrightarrow{Heat} 2MgO(s)$

When aluminium is heated with iron oxide, the aluminium is oxidised to produce aluminium oxide and the iron oxide is reduced to iron.

| Aluminium | + | Iron oxide | Heat → | Aluminium oxide | + | Iron |

(HT) $2Al(s) + Fe_2O_3(s) \xrightarrow{Heat} Al_2O_3(s) + 2Fe(s)$

Key Words

Combustion • Dilute • Insoluble salt • Neutralisation • Oxidation • Precipitate • Reduction • Salt • Soluble salt

Making Salts

A **neutral salt** is formed when an acid reacts with a base. This type of reaction is called **neutralisation**. Most salts formed from this reaction are **soluble**.

Dilute acids react with metal hydroxides to form a salt and water.

Dilute acids react with metal oxides to form a salt and water.

Dilute acids react with metal carbonates to form a salt, water and carbon dioxide.

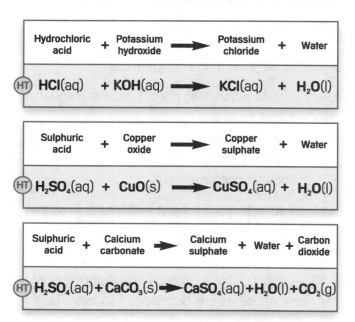

| Hydrochloric acid | + | Potassium hydroxide | → | Potassium chloride | + | Water |

(HT) $HCl(aq) + KOH(aq) \longrightarrow KCl(aq) + H_2O(l)$

| Sulphuric acid | + | Copper oxide | → | Copper sulphate | + | Water |

(HT) $H_2SO_4(aq) + CuO(s) \longrightarrow CuSO_4(aq) + H_2O(l)$

| Sulphuric acid | + | Calcium carbonate | → | Calcium sulphate | + | Water | + | Carbon dioxide |

(HT) $H_2SO_4(aq) + CaCO_3(s) \longrightarrow CaSO_4(aq) + H_2O(l) + CO_2(g)$

Types of Salts

The salt produced depends on the acid and metal used:

- Sulphuric acid produces sulphate salts.
- Hydrochloric acid produces chloride salts.

Some salts formed during neutralisation are **insoluble salts**.

A **precipitate** is formed when two **soluble salt** solutions are mixed together.

The pure salt can be retrieved using this method:

1. Filter off the acid.
2. Wash it with distilled water.
3. Dry it in a warm oven.

Salts can be used…

- as fertilisers
- as colouring agents in fireworks
- for colouring glass, enamels, paints and dyes
- as an addition to fuel to improve **combustion** and reduce pollutants.

Hazard Labels

Symbols are used to identify chemical hazards:

- Toxic substances can kill.
- Oxidising substances cause substances to burn more fiercely.
- Harmful substances are similar to toxic substances but are less dangerous.
- Flammable substances catch fire easily.
- Corrosive substances attack other materials and living tissue.
- Irritant substances may cause skin to blister.

Toxic

Oxidising

Harmful

Flammable

Corrosive

Irritant

Making Changes

Chemical Substances

Chemical substances can be…

- **natural**
- **artificial** (man-made or synthetic).

Using natural substances doesn't always mean that they're better for you:

- Henna tattoos can cause allergic reactions.
- Untreated water can kill.
- Rotting fruit contains toxins.

Artificial substances are **more reliable** because they have been made with a specific composition in a controlled environment.

Artificial substances are chemically designed to be the same as the natural substances so often it's difficult to see the differences between them.

Chemical	Natural / Artificial	Effect
Histamine	Natural	Inflammation or anaphylactic shock
Anti-histamine	Artificial	Reduces mild irritation and inflammation caused by histamine
Foxglove flowers	Natural	Poisonous – could kill
Digitalis	Artificial	Extracted from foxglove flowers in the lab and used to treat heart conditions

Chemical Reactions in Cooking

Cooking food is the process of using heat to create products through a variety of chemical reactions.

When heated, food may undergo changes in…

- appearance
- flavour
- texture.

Baking powder contains **sodium hydrogencarbonate** and an acidic substance. It's used to create baked goods that rise and have a delicate structure (e.g. muffins).

Baking powder works in the following way:

1. Carbon dioxide bubbles are released when it reacts with acidic substances.
2. When the mixture is heated, larger bubbles are released, creating further lift in the baked product.
3. Once it's cooked, the air pockets are fixed in position and the product can't rise any more.

HT Some chemical substances that are added to food result in **adverse side effects**.

For example, scientific research may have linked **additives** to **hyperactivity** in children. A recent report suggested that if additives were taken out of children's food, hyperactivity cases would go down. But, it also suggested that the additives may not always be responsible for hyperactivity.

Key Words

Carbohydrate • Caustic soda • Citric acid • Decomposition • Dehydration • Hydration • Thermal decomposition

Thermal Decomposition

When hydrogencarbonates and carbonates are heated, they release carbon dioxide. This is called **thermal decomposition**.

For example, when you heat calcium hydrogencarbonate, it **decomposes** into calcium carbonate, carbon dioxide and water.

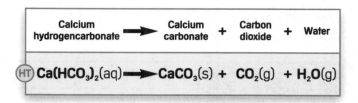

Calcium hydrogencarbonate ⟶ Calcium carbonate + Carbon dioxide + Water

(HT) $Ca(HCO_3)_2(aq) \longrightarrow CaCO_3(s) + CO_2(g) + H_2O(g)$

Hydration and Dehydration

Blue crystals of hydrated copper sulphate become white anhydrous copper sulphate on heating, as **water is removed**. This is a **dehydration** reaction.

This reaction is reversible. If **water is added** to the white anhydrous copper sulphate, blue hydrated copper sulphate is formed. This is called a **hydration** reaction.

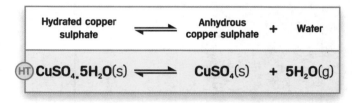

Hydrated copper sulphate ⇌ Anhydrous copper sulphate + Water

(HT) $CuSO_4.5H_2O(s) \rightleftharpoons CuSO_4(s) + 5H_2O(g)$

Common Compounds

Compounds are formed when two or more elements join together as a result of a chemical reaction. This table shows the uses of common compounds.

Compound	Uses	Compound	Uses
Citric acid	To make soft drinks, laxatives and cathartics.	Ethanoic (acetic) acid	To preserve food, as vinegar and to make plastics.
Ammonia	To make fertilisers, dyes and paints.	Hydrochloric acid	To make chlorides and to process glucose.
Carbohydrates	To make fats, fabrics and adhesives.	Phosphoric acid	For cleaning and to make jellies and beverages.
Carbon dioxide	To make carbonated drinks, aspirin and fire extinguishers.	Sodium chloride (table salt)	As a seasoning, in chemical production and to make soap.
Caustic soda (sodium hydroxide)	To make paper, textiles and soaps, and in the manufacture of other chemicals.	Water	As steam to turn turbines in power stations and as a lubricant when cutting materials.

Making Changes

Collecting Gases

This table shows the different ways that you could collect gases.

Method	Downward delivery	Upward delivery	Over water	Gas syringe
When Used	When the gas is heavier than air.	When the gas is lighter than air.	When the gas is sparingly soluble in water.	When you want to measure the volume of gas produced.
Apparatus	Gas jar	Gas jar	Gas jar	Gas syringe

Testing Gases

This table shows how to test for gases.

Gas	Ammonia, NH_3	Oxygen, O_2	Hydrogen, H_2	Chlorine, Cl_2	Carbon dioxide, CO_2
Properties	A colourless, alkaline gas with a pungent smell.	A colourless gas that helps fuels burn more readily in air.	A colourless gas that combines violently with oxygen when ignited.	A green, poisonous gas that bleaches dyes.	A colourless, mildly acidic gas that turns limewater milky.
Test	Turns damp indicator paper blue.	Relights a glowing splint.	Burns with a squeaky pop.	Turns damp indicator paper white.	Turns limewater cloudy/milky.

Glossary of Key Words

Carbohydrates – chemical compounds of carbon, hydrogen and oxygen, such as sugars and starches.

Caustic soda – the common name for sodium hydroxide; a strong alkali used to make chemicals and soaps; very corrosive.

Citric acid – a weak acid that can be found in all citrus fruits, which is soluble in water.

Combustion – a chemical reaction that occurs when fuels burn, releasing heat.

Decomposition – the process by which a substance is broken down into simpler substances.

Dehydration – the removal of the elements of water from a substance.

Dilute – the process of adding water / solvent to a solution to make it weaker / less concentrated.

Hydration – the addition of water to a substance.

Insoluble salt – a solid that will not dissolve in a liquid.

Neutralisation – a reaction between an acid and a base, which forms products that are pH neutral.

Oxidation – a reaction that involves the gain of oxygen or the loss of electrons.

Precipitate – an insoluble solid formed during a reaction involving solutions.

Reduction – a reaction that involves the loss of oxygen or the gain of electrons.

Salt – the product of a chemical reaction; formed when hydrogen is displaced from an acid.

Soluble salt – a salt that will easily dissolve in a liquid.

Thermal decomposition – using heat to break down a large molecule into smaller molecules or atoms.

Practice Questions

1 Number the following metals **1–4** to show the correct order of reactivity, starting with the most reactive.

A Sodium ☐   **B** Gold ☐

C Zinc ☐   **D** Aluminium ☐

2 The method of extracting a metal from its ore depends on the metal's position in what?

....

3 Which of the following statements describe what happens during reduction and oxidation? Tick the correct option(s).

A Reduction is the gain of oxygen. ☐   **B** Oxidation is the gain of oxygen. ☐

C Reduction is the loss of oxygen. ☐   **D** Oxidation is the loss of oxygen. ☐

4 What is neutralisation?

....

5 a) What products are formed when copper oxide reacts with sulphuric acid?

....

b) What products are formed when hydrochloric acid reacts with calcium carbonate?

....

6 Give three uses of salts.

a) ....   **b)** ....   **c)** ....

7 Draw lines between the boxes to match each substance to the description of its hazard.

Irritant	Cause other substances to burn more fiercely
Oxidising	Can cause skin to blister
Toxic	Attack other materials and living tissue
Flammable	Catch fire easily
Corrosive	Can kill

8 What is the difference between natural and artificial substances?

....

....

9 Circle the correct options in the following sentences.

Cooking food is the process of using **cold** / **heat** to create **products** / **reactants** through a variety of chemical reactions. It results in a change in **appearance** / **quality**, flavour and texture.

10 Which gas is released from baking powder to create a delicate structure in baked goods?

....

11 What is the name of the process that breaks down a compound using heat?

....

12 Describe what happens when blue crystals of copper sulphate are heated and then have water added to them.

....

....

....

13 List three uses of the following compounds.

a) Sodium chloride

i) .... **ii)** .... **iii)** ....

b) Carbohydrates

i) .... **ii)** .... **iii)** ....

c) Ethanoic acid

i) .... **ii)** .... **iii)** ....

14 Are the following statements **true** or **false**?

a) Chlorine turns damp indicator paper blue. ....

b) Ammonia is a colourless gas with a pungent smell. ....

c) Carbon dioxide is a colourless, slightly acidic gas. ....

There's One Earth

The Atmosphere

The **atmosphere** has changed a lot since the formation of the Earth 4.6 billion years ago.

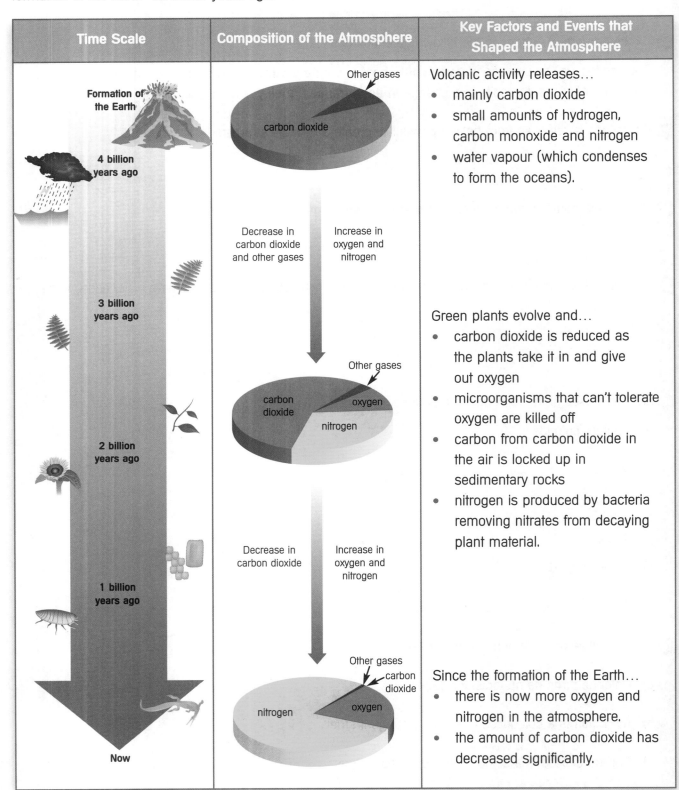

Time Scale	Composition of the Atmosphere	Key Factors and Events that Shaped the Atmosphere
Formation of the Earth 4 billion years ago	Other gases carbon dioxide	Volcanic activity releases… • mainly carbon dioxide • small amounts of hydrogen, carbon monoxide and nitrogen • water vapour (which condenses to form the oceans).
	Decrease in carbon dioxide and other gases Increase in oxygen and nitrogen	
3 billion years ago 2 billion years ago	Other gases carbon dioxide oxygen nitrogen	Green plants evolve and… • carbon dioxide is reduced as the plants take it in and give out oxygen • microorganisms that can't tolerate oxygen are killed off • carbon from carbon dioxide in the air is locked up in sedimentary rocks • nitrogen is produced by bacteria removing nitrates from decaying plant material.
	Decrease in carbon dioxide Increase in oxygen and nitrogen	
1 billion years ago Now	Other gases carbon dioxide nitrogen oxygen	Since the formation of the Earth… • there is now more oxygen and nitrogen in the atmosphere. • the amount of carbon dioxide has decreased significantly.

Global Warming

Global warming is the **increase in temperature** of the surface of the Earth.

In the early 20th Century, a Swedish chemist predicted that carbon dioxide levels in the atmosphere would double within 3000 years, resulting in a global temperature increase of 5°C.

By the 1960s and 1970s the opposite was thought to be happening: global cooling.

By the late 1970s and mid-1980s, **computer-simulated models** were predicting an increase in the Earth's temperature and a doubling of the level of carbon dioxide within a century. But, there are always uncertainties with computer simulations.

By the late 1980s the theory of global warming was widely accepted as a result of scientific findings.

N.B. You should be able to use the internet to find up-to-date information about global warming.

Causes of Global Warming

An increase in levels of greenhouse gases causes an increase in the Earth's temperature as greenhouse gases prevent heat from leaving the Earth's atmosphere.

Industrialisation has caused an increase in levels of greenhouse gases. The gases are the result of…

- the burning of **fossil fuels** (oil, coal, gas), which produces carbon dioxide, sulphur dioxide (which contributes to **acid rain**) and carbon monoxide.
- motorised **transportation**
- an increase in **cattle farming** and **rice growing**
- the use of **CFCs** (chlorofluorocarbons)
- **deforestation**.

HT Combating Global Warming

Although it's impossible to stop global warming, there are ways of combating its effects:
- Invest in and use renewable energy.
- Meet the Kyoto protocol.
- Use geo-engineering for plankton growth.

All the methods of combating global warming are based on the **precautionary principle**: if we are not completely certain about the effects of something, we should act to prevent it.

Key Words

Acid rain • Fossil fuel • Global warming

There's One Earth

Fractional Distillation of Crude Oil

Crude oil is a mixture of **hydrocarbons**. A hydrocarbon is a compound that contains only hydrogen and carbon atoms.

Crude oil can be separated into different **fractions** (parts) by **fractional distillation**. Each fraction contains hydrocarbon molecules with a **similar number** of carbon atoms.

The process takes place in a **fractionating column**:

1. The oil is evaporated by heating.
2. It's allowed to condense at a range of different temperatures.
3. Fractions with **low boiling points** and **viscosity** exit towards the top of the column.
4. Fractions with **high boiling points** and viscosity exit towards the bottom of the column.

Cool

Short-chain hydrocarbons

Long-chain hydrocarbons

Crude oil vapour

Hot

25°C → **Refinery gases** – e.g. propane and butane for bottled gases.

70°C → **Gasoline (petrol)** – fuel for cars.

180°C → **Naphtha** – used for medicines, cosmetics, chemicals and plastics.

260°C → **Kerosene (paraffin)** – fuel for jet aircraft.

300°C → **Diesel oil (gas oil)** – fuel for transport.

340°C → **Lubricating oil**

360°C → **Fuel oil** – fuel for heating systems and some power stations.

over 400°C → **Bitumen** – to make roads.

HT The greater the number of carbon atoms in a hydrocarbon...

- the more viscous it is
- the higher its boiling point
- the less volatile and flammable it is.

Hydrocarbon	N° Carbon Atoms	Hydrocarbon	N° Carbon Atoms
Refinery gases	1–4	Diesel oil	15–22
Gasoline	5–6	Lubricating oil	20–30
Naphtha	6–10	Fuel oil	30–40
Kerosene	10–16	Bitumen	50+

Fractional Distillation of Air

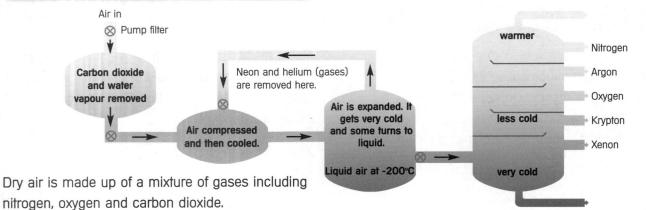

Air in
⊗ Pump filter

Carbon dioxide and water vapour removed

Air compressed and then cooled.

Neon and helium (gases) are removed here.

Air is expanded. It gets very cold and some turns to liquid.

Liquid air at -200°C

warmer

less cold

very cold

Nitrogen

Argon

Oxygen

Krypton

Xenon

Dry air is made up of a mixture of gases including nitrogen, oxygen and carbon dioxide.

Oxygen and nitrogen can be obtained by separating them from liquid air through **fractional distillation**.

Combustion of Fuels

A fuel is a substance that releases useful amounts of energy when burned. Many fuels are hydrocarbons.

When a fuel burns, it reacts with oxygen from the air. This is called **combustion**. The fuel has be **ignited** before it can react with oxygen.

Complete Combustion

Complete combustion happens when there's plenty of oxygen available. Complete combustion of a hydrocarbon produces carbon dioxide and water, and energy is released.

Methane	+	Oxygen	⟶	Carbon dioxide	+	Water

(HT) $CH_4(g) + 2O_2(g) \longrightarrow CO_2(g) + 2H_2O(g)$

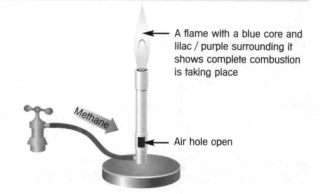

A flame with a blue core and lilac / purple surrounding it shows complete combustion is taking place

Air hole open

Incomplete Combustion

Incomplete combustion happens when a fuel burns without sufficient oxygen. Incomplete combustion of a hydrocarbon produces carbon monoxide:

Methane	+	Oxygen	⟶	Carbon monoxide	+	Water

(HT) $2CH_4(g) + 3O_2(g) \longrightarrow 2CO(g) + 4H_2O(g)$

Incomplete combustion in faulty gas appliances and other heating appliances can produce carbon monoxide. This can be dangerous.

If there's very little oxygen available when a hydrocarbon is burned, carbon is produced. A **sooty**, yellow flame is an indication of incomplete combustion because it contains carbon. With less oxygen, heat energy decreases and pollutants and **residue** increase.

Methane	+	Oxygen	⟶	Carbon	+	Water

(HT) $CH_4(g) + O_2(g) \longrightarrow C(s) + 2H_2O(g)$

Yellow flame shows incomplete combustion is taking place

Air hole closed

Key Words

Combustion • Complete combustion • Crude oil • Fractional distillation • Fractionating column • Hydrocarbon • Ignition • Incomplete combustion • Residue • Sootiness • Viscosity

There's One Earth

Pollutants

Although **hydrocarbons** produce useful amounts of energy when they burn, the gases they produce are pollutants because they contain particulates:

- Carbon dioxide increases the Greenhouse Effect and contributes to **global warming**.
- Carbon monoxide is a **toxic**, colourless and odourless gas that reduces the ability of blood to carry oxygen.

(HT) Other pollutants produced from burning fuels can have a serious impact on health and are thought to cause illnesses, e.g. asthma (which is more prevalent in developed countries).

Alternatives to Fossil Fuels

Bio-fuels are an attractive alternative to **fossil fuels**. These are fuels based on **sustainable** resources, e.g. animal waste, organic household waste, wood and alcohol.

Ethanol is a bio-fuel that is produced by fermentation of sugar beet and sugar cane. Ethanol can reduce the demand for petrol, however, large areas of fertile land have to be used to grow the crops.

Volume for volume, ethanol produces less carbon dioxide and water than methane.

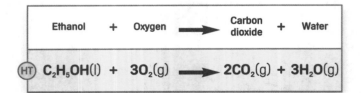

Ethanol	+	Oxygen	→	Carbon dioxide	+	Water

(HT) $C_2H_5OH(l) + 3O_2(g) \longrightarrow 2CO_2(g) + 3H_2O(g)$

Hydrogen fuel can be used in cars instead of petrol and it has many benefits:

- It's the cleanest of all the fuels as it only produces water.
- It can supply three times the energy of petrol.

But, it also has many drawbacks:

- New cars would be needed because of the technology used to get electricity from the hydrogen.
- Producing the hydrogen may involve the use of fossil fuels so could still add to pollution.

Recycling

When something that's no longer needed is **recycled**, another use for it is found and the planet's resources are conserved.

The most common materials that are recycled are…
* metals
* paper
* glass.

Metals, when they are recycled, will use between $\frac{1}{20}$ and $\frac{1}{3}$ of the energy than when first extracted. Aluminium and steel are currently the easiest metals to recycle.

Recycling paper uses less water and energy than were used to produce it in the first place, and releases less methane into the atmosphere.

Glass will not rot away. If it's recycled it takes 20% less energy than it did to make it in the first place and the process produces 20% less pollution.

Economics and the Environment

Recycling makes **environmental sense** because…
* it saves on raw materials
* it saves on landfill sites and other costs associated with waste disposal
* reusing materials often requires less energy than extracting new materials
* it cuts down on excavation and mining so there's less environmental damage and fewer waste products
* it uses less water and chemical substances so reduces pollution.

In industry, many companies make decisions about recycling based on cost, i.e. they are more likely to recycle materials if it saves / makes them money.

Sustainable development is concerned with balancing the need for economic development, standards of living and respect for the environment, without compromising future generations.

Sustainable resources are resources that can be maintained in the long term at a level that allows appropriate use by people.

Desalination involves removing salt from salt water (e.g. sea water) to produce drinking water. It's used when the demand for fresh water is greater than the available supply.

Key Words

Bio-fuel • Desalination • Recycle • Sustainability • Toxic

There's One Earth

Making Useful Substances

Salt and other useful products are taken from sea water in the following way:

① The sea water is evaporated in wide, shallow ponds to produce solar salt.

② The solar salt is turned into saturated brine (concentrated sodium chloride solution).

③ Saturated brine is boiled in vacuum pans to purify it.

④ The brine is left to evaporate leaving salt crystals.

Salt and other useful products can also be taken from rock salt (sodium chloride):

① Rock salt is generally mined from the ground.

② A process is then used, which is similar to the process used to obtain salt from sea water.

The salt obtained from these processes is used in food products. However, the brine can be separated into other useful products.

Electrolysis of Sodium Chloride

Sodium chloride (table salt) is used as a seasoning and preservative for foods, for making pottery, soap, glass and textile dyes, and in the production of chemical substances.

If a direct current is passed through a concentrated solution of sodium chloride (rock salt), three main products are obtained:

* **Chlorine** at the positive electrode. This is used for making chemical substances, bleaches, disinfectants, paints and plastics.

* **Hydrogen** at the negative electrode. This is used for manufacturing margarine and ammonia.

* **Sodium hydroxide** remains in the solution and is used for making soap, paper and synthetic fibres.

Sodium is obtained by electrolysis of molten sodium chloride. This process also produces chlorine. Sodium is used in street lamps and in nuclear reactors (transferring heat from the reactor to the steam generators).

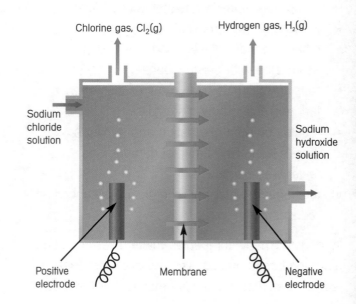

Chlorine gas, $Cl_2(g)$ Hydrogen gas, $H_2(g)$

Sodium chloride solution

Sodium hydroxide solution

Positive electrode   Membrane   Negative electrode

Glossary of Key Words

Acid rain – rain containing sulphur dioxide and nitrogen oxides.

Bio-fuel – a source of renewable energy made from biological materials that include plants and animal waste.

Combustion – a chemical reaction that occurs when substances burn, releasing heat.

Complete combustion – (of hydrocarbons) the production of carbon dioxide and water through the burning of a hydrocarbon in the presence of oxygen.

Crude oil – a liquid mixture found in rocks, which contains hydrocarbons.

Desalination – the process of removing salt from water.

Fossil fuel – fuel formed in the ground, over millions of years, from the remains of dead plants or animals.

Fractional distillation – the process used to separate crude oil into groups of hydrocarbons with similar boiling points, called fractions.

Fractionating column – the equipment used to separate a mixture of liquids.

Global warming – the gradual increase in the average temperature on Earth.

Hydrocarbon – a compound made of carbon and hydrogen atoms only.

Ignition – the means by which combustion is started.

Incomplete combustion – this will happen if there is not enough oxygen when a fuel is being burned. In hydrocarbons, it results in a sooty flame, carbon monoxide, carbon as soot and water being produced.

Recycle – re-use materials that would otherwise be considered waste.

Residue – the substance that remains after a chemical reaction or a process.

Sootiness – the amount of carbon particles present in a flame: the more carbon particles there are, the greater the sootiness.

Sustainability – the ability to meet the needs of the current generation without affecting the needs of future generations.

Toxic – a poisonous substance.

Viscosity – how easily a liquid can flow / be poured: if a liquid is highly viscous it is difficult to pour, e.g. treacle.

Practice Questions

1 List three ways in which the evolution of plants has affected the atmosphere.

a) ....

b) ....

c) ....

2 In the late 1970s to the mid-1980s, what did computer-simulated models predict about the level of carbon dioxide in the atmosphere within the next century? Tick the correct option.

A It would triple ☐   **B** It would halve ☐

C It would decrease ☐   **D** It would double ☐

3 What contributes to global warming?

....

....

4 What processes form greenhouse gases? Tick the correct option(s).

A Deforestation ☐   **B** Not burning fossil fuels ☐

C Increase in cattle farming ☐   **D** Decrease in rice growing ☐

HT

5 Give two ways of combating the effects of global warming.

a) ....

b) ....

6 What is the precautionary principle?

....

....

7 List two changes in hydrocarbons as the number of carbon atoms per molecule increases.

a) ....

b) ....

8 a) Name three gases that are found in dry air.

i) .... ii) .... iii) ....

b) How are oxygen and nitrogen in air separated?

....

9 Circle the correct options in the following sentences.

a) Complete combustion occurs when there's **little** / **plenty** of oxygen.

b) When fuels react with **oxygen** / **hydrogen** from the air they **react** / **burn**, releasing useful amounts of **energy** / **sparks**.

c) Incomplete combustion occurs when a fuel **burns** / **reacts** without sufficient oxygen and will produce carbon **monoxide** / **dioxide**.

10 What are the drawbacks of using hydrogen fuel? Tick the correct option(s).

A New cars would be needed ⬭

B It's a clean fuel ⬭

C It supplies three times the energy of petrol ⬭

D It might need fossil fuels to produce it ⬭

E Large areas of fertile land have to be used ⬭

F It could still add to levels of pollution ⬭

11 Which three materials are the most common materials to be recycled?

a) .... **b)** .... **c)** ....

12 How is sodium metal obtained?

....

13 What three main products are obtained when a direct electric current is passed through a concentrated solution of sodium chloride?

a) ....

b) ....

c) ....

Designer Products

Smart Materials

Smart materials are materials that are able to change their properties in response to an external stimulus, for example…

- heat
- light
- atmospheric conditions.

Fabrics made from smart materials are designed to maximise characteristics, e.g. **breathability**.

They are usually manufactured using **microfibres** (very thin fibres of polymers) and have a variety of uses.

Smart Material	Information	Uses
Carbon fibre	<ul><li>Carbon fibre strands or carbon fibre fabric are used to reinforce various polymers.</li><li>Products made from carbon fibres are very light and very strong.</li><li>Some products are designed to be more flexible than metals.</li></ul>	<ul><li>Tennis rackets</li><li>Hockey sticks</li><li>Snowboards</li><li>Paddles for water sports</li><li>Bicycles</li></ul>
Thinsulate™	<ul><li>Thinsulate™ is a unique insulation material made from microfibres. The microfibres trap more air than conventional fleece materials.</li><li>Thinsulate™ is a thin, warm, breathable, washable and dry-cleanable material.</li><li>Thinsulate™ is moisture-resistant and can keep you warm even when it's damp.</li></ul>	<ul><li>Outdoor clothing</li><li>Dive-wear</li><li>Ski-wear</li><li>Mountaineering-wear</li><li>Cycle-wear</li></ul>
Lycra™	<ul><li>Lycra™ is a unique man-made elastic fibre, also known as spandex.</li><li>It's knitted or woven with other fabrics such as cotton, wool, silk and nylon.</li><li>Lycra™ stretches so produces fabrics and garments that are comfortable, fit well, and provide freedom of movement.</li></ul>	<ul><li>Swimwear</li><li>Underwear</li><li>Workout wear</li><li>Running shorts</li><li>Cycling shorts</li></ul>

Designed Materials

The uses of some materials with novel properties only become apparent after they have been developed:

- **Post-its®** use a special sticky material that was first discovered in 1968. But it was six years before they were developed. They are now used worldwide.
- **Teflon**™ was discovered in 1938 when a compressed sample of tetrafluoroethene was found to have spontaneously polymerised into PTFE (polytetrafluoroethene). Teflon™ is inert (unreactive) and slippery, and is used as non-stick coating in cookware.

Kevlar™ and Gore-Tex™

The unique properties of **Kevlar**™ come from the way the chains of polymer lie together within the structure of the material.

Kevlar™ is…
- very strong and lightweight
- hard to break
- resistant to chemicals, cutting and fire.

Kevlar™ has many uses because of its properties, including personal body armour, skis, helmets, and aerospace and fire-protective clothing.

Gore-Tex™ is **breathable** because a **hydrophilic** ('water loving') substance is added to the structure that allows moisture to pass through. Gore-Tex™ is used to make all-weather clothing and shoes.

HT Designing New Products

An important part of product design is analysing how the product will be used and identifying the properties it will need in order to work well:
- Some properties are essential for the product to fulfil its purpose.
- Other properties enhance the product and make it more desirable or useful.

For example, windproof gloves for walkers must keep the wind out. But, there are other properties that will make them more comfortable to wear and more user friendly, e.g. being breathable, lightweight, flexible, warm, soft to the touch, and washable.

Key Words

Breathability • Carbon fibre • Gore-Tex™ **• Kevlar**™ **• Lycra**™ **• Smart material • Teflon**™ **• Thinsulate**™

Designer Products

Nanotechnology

Nanotechnology involves the study and use of microscopically small pieces of material. On this tiny scale, materials have much better properties.

Nanomaterials can be stronger and lighter than conventional materials, and can conduct heat or electricity in different ways.

Nanoparticles are incredibly tiny particles that have special applications. For example, tiny particles of titanium dioxide added to suntan lotions are transparent on the skin and can absorb or reflect UV radiation.

Nanocomposites

Nanocomposites can be made from clay and **polymer**, metal and polymer, or carbon nanotube and **polymer**.

The use of nanomaterials in composites results in materials with many **improved properties**, for example…
- improved strength and thermal stability
- decreased permeability to liquids and gases
- flame retardancy
- improved electrical conductivity and chemical resistance.

Future Uses of Nanocomposites

Scientists are looking at what else they can use nanoparticles for, including…
- new generation army uniforms and equipment
- filters that can sterilise a range of drugs
- self-cleaning shoes, clothes, kitchen surfaces and bathroom tiles.

Nanotechnology has lots of potential and is mostly aimed at **medical uses**. For example, scientists are working on medical nanosensors that can be placed in cells to detect changes in levels of chemical substances. This could be useful for studying diseases and general conditions.

HT Although nanotechnology has great potential, there are **social and ethical issues** with any future uses of nanotechnology:
- Personal security and safety may be better due to the use of small sensors and computers. But this could lead to the same technology being used to spy on people.
- Nanosensors could be used by the military to detect chemical and biological weapons. But some people think they could be used to create new threats.
- Nanorobots could repair human bodies at the cellular level. But people are worried that this is too unnatural.

Intelligent Packaging

Intelligent packaging has been specially developed to have properties that are desirable to the consumer. It's used to keep food fresh.

The **'oxygen scavenger'** is an atmosphere controller. It removes oxygen from inside the package, preventing the decay of food. This is done by using a small sachet filled with modified iron(II) carbonate.

The **'bullseye' label** is a time-temperature indicator. Consumers can see from the colour of the label whether the food has been kept at a warm temperature for too long.

Water in packaging can be minimised by the **absorption of liquid water**, or **humidity buffering**. Drip-absorbent sheets absorb liquid water. Humidity buffering reduces the humidity inside food packages.

Fermentation

Yeast is used to convert **sugar** into **ethanol** and carbon dioxide. This is called **fermentation**.

The ethanol produced during fermentation is used to make beer and wine.

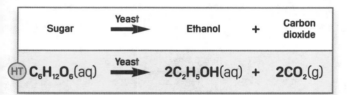

Sugar	$\xrightarrow{\text{Yeast}}$	Ethanol	+	Carbon dioxide
HT $C_6H_{12}O_6$(aq)	$\xrightarrow{\text{Yeast}}$	$2C_2H_5OH$(aq)	+	$2CO_2$(g)

Effects of Alcohol

Ethanol is the **alcohol** that is found in alcoholic drinks. It can have many harmful effects on the body, including…

- a deficiency in vitamin B causing skin damage, diarrhoea and depression
- decreased levels of iron, leading to anaemia
- liver damage
- destruction of brain cells
- an increased risk of heart disease and high blood pressure.

There has been an increase in cases of binge drinking in the UK in recent years. Binge drinking has many social implications.

For example…
- hangovers
- mood changes
- people finding themselves in violent situations
- increased risk of accidents
- lowered inhibitions and greater risk of getting into trouble.

Key Words

Alcohol • Ethanol • Fermentation • Nanocomposites • Nanoparticles • Nanotechnology • Polymer • Sugar

Designer Products

Emulsifiers

An **emulsifier** is an additive that is put in food to stop mixtures of oils and water-based liquids from separating.

Normally oil and water don't mix, but when an emulsifier is added to the mixture, an emulsion is formed, e.g. mayonnaise. An emulsion can either be oil-in-water or water-in-oil:

- An **oil-in-water emulsion** contains small droplets of oil that are dispersed in water.
- A **water-in-oil emulsion** contains small droplets of water that are dispersed in oil.

How Emulsifiers Work

Emulsifiers are molecules that have two different ends:
- One end is **hydrophobic** ('water hating').
- One end is **hydrophilic** ('water loving').

In oil-in-water emulsions…
- the hydrophobic end hates water but loves oil so it will coat the oil molecules
- the oil molecules become insulated from the water, preventing the emulsion from separating.

In water-in-oil emulsions…
- the hydrophilic end hates oil but loves water so it will coat the water molecules
- the water molecules become insulated from the oil, preventing the emulsion from separating.

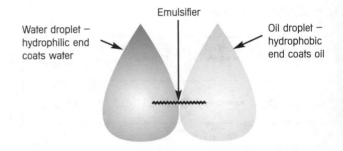
Water droplet – hydrophilic end coats water | Emulsifier | Oil droplet – hydrophobic end coats oil

An Emulsion

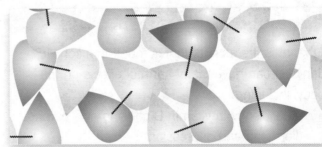

Uses of Emulsifiers in Food

Emulsifiers are used in…
- bread
- low-fat spreads
- ice cream and spray cream
- sponge cakes and chocolate.

Key Words
Emulsifier • Hydrophilic • Hydrophobic

Glossary of Key Words

Alcohol – a colourless, flammable liquid that contains carbon, hydrogen and oxygen. It contains an –OH or hydroxyl group.

Breathability – the ability of a material to allow sweat vapours to escape from the inside of the fabric to the outside.

Carbon fibre – a strong, stiff, thin fibre of nearly pure carbon which, when combined with other materials, produces a strong, lightweight material.

Emulsifier – an additive that will stop two liquids from separating when they are mixed together, especially if those liquids wouldn't normally mix together.

Ethanol – the product of fermentation; a clear, colourless alcohol solution found in beverages such as wine, beer and brandy. The formula of its molecules is: C_2H_5OH.

Fermentation – the process in which enzymes in yeast turn sugars (in particular glucose) into ethanol and carbon dioxide, without the need for oxygen gas.

Gore-Tex™ – a brand of weatherproof membrane that allows small sweat particles to pass out from the body, whilst preventing rain and wind from entering.

Hydrophilic – a substance that attracts water, absorbs water or dissolves in water.

Hydrophobic – a substance that repels or 'hates' water, but attracts oil.

Kevlar™ – a brand of aramid fibre that is strong, lightweight and flexible. It's often used to make bullet-resistant and stab-resistant vests.

Lycra™ – a synthetic fibre made from a long-chain polymer that has stretch and recovery properties giving comfort, fit and freedom of movement.

Nanocomposites – composite materials made from particles less than 100 nanometres in size. They are materials that offer greater strength, wear and corrosion resistance than more traditional composites.

Nanoparticles – very small particles that have at least one dimension less than 100 nanometres.

Nanotechnology – working with matter on an ultra-small scale in areas including medicine, physics, chemistry and engineering.

Polymer – a long-chain hydrocarbon (compound of hydrogen and carbon); a plastic e,g, PVC, PTFE etc.

Smart material – a material that senses its environment and responds to it.

Sugar – a carbohydrate that is readily soluble in water. It is made during photosynthesis in plants and is found in many animals. It can also be turned into ethanol by enzymes in yeast.

Teflon™ – a brand of polymer called PTFE (polytetrafluoroethene); a slippery, non-stick material best-known for coating cookware.

Thinsulate™ – a brand of thin, breathable fabric that is moisture-resistant and able to retain warmth whilst damp.

Practice Questions

1 How do smart materials behave?

....

....

2 What is Lycra™?

....

3 When do the uses of some materials with novel properties become apparent?

....

4 What are the unique properties of Kevlar™ that make it a useful material?

a) ....

b) ....

c) ....

HT

5 An important part of designing a new product is analysing how well it will work, but what else is involved? Tick the correct option(s).

A   Identifying properties it needs to have in order to work well   ☐

B   Analysing how much it will eventually cost   ☐

C   Identifying properties essential to fulfil its purpose   ☐

D   Identifying properties that enhance the product so it's more desirable   ☐

E   Analysing how easy it is to make the product   ☐

6 How have windproof gloves been designed to make them more comfortable to wear and more user friendly?

....

....

7 What is the name of the technology that involves the study and use of microscopically small materials?

....

8 Give four properties that can be improved by using nanomaterials in composites.

a) ....

b) ....

c) ....

d) ....

HT

9 Give one social or ethical issue associated with using nanosensors in the future.

....

....

10 How is water in food packaging minimised?

....

....

11 What is the name of the process that involves yeast converting sugar into ethanol?

....

12 Ethanol is a form of alcohol found in alcoholic drinks.
List three possible harmful effects it could have on your body.

a) ....

b) ....

c) ....

13 An emulsifier is an additive that is put in food to stop emulsions from separating. Which of the following is a type of emulsion? Tick the correct option.

A Oil-in-fat ⬭   **B** Water-in-fat ⬭   **C** Oil-in-water ⬭   **D** Oil-in-solution ⬭

14 Name three foods in which emulsifiers are used.

a) ....   b) ....   c) ....

Producing and Measuring Electricity

Current

Current is the rate of flow of electrons in a component. **Electrons** have a negative charge. In a complete circuit, they leave the **negative** terminal because they're attracted towards the positive terminal (although circuit diagrams show the flow the opposite way).

The greater the flow of electrons (i.e. the more electrons per second) the greater the current.

The current in a wire can be measured by placing an ammeter in series in the circuit. The symbol for an ammeter is —(A)—.

Direct Current and Alternating Current

Direct current (DC) flows in **one** direction only:

- Circuit **1** shows a circuit with a DC source. Arrows are used to show direct current flowing from positive to negative.
- The trace for DC on a cathode ray oscilloscope is also shown.

Alternating current (AC) **oscillates** (reverses its direction) continuously:

- Circuit **2** shows a circuit with an AC source. The direction of AC can't be shown because it's always changing.
- The trace for AC on a cathode ray oscilloscope is also shown.

Mains electricity is AC. It has a frequency of 50 **hertz** (50Hz), which means it oscillates 50 times each second.

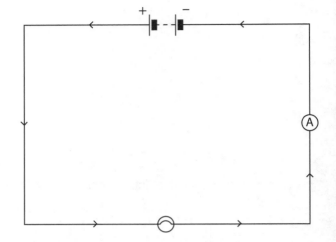

Direct Current

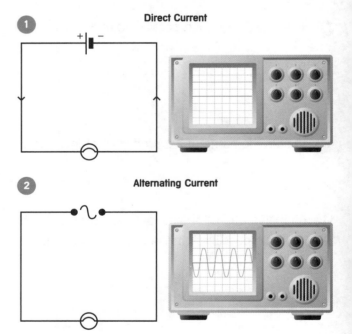

Alternating Current

Sources of Direct Current

The following are all sources of direct current:
- **Cells** / batteries.
- Solar cells – produce a direct current using the Sun's light energy.
- **Generators** – use the principle of rotating coils of wire in a magnetic field to generate electricity.

Key Words

Ammeter • Amp-hour • Battery • Capacity • Current • Dry cell • Rechargeable • Solar cell

Producing and Measuring Electricity

Cells (Batteries)

There are three main types of cell:

Type	Contents	Use
Wet cell **rechargeable**	Lead and acid	Cars, industry
Dry cell non-rechargeable	Zinc, carbon, manganese, mercury or lithium	Torches, clocks, radios, hearing aids, pacemakers
Dry cell rechargeable	Nickel, cadmium, lithium	Mobile phones, power tools

Non-rechargeable cells are harmful to the environment because…

- the energy needed to make a cell is 50 times greater than the energy it produces
- less than 5% of dry cells are recycled (compared to 90% of wet-cell car batteries)
- the UK produces about 30 000 tonnes of waste dry cells every year (more than 20 cells per household)
- toxic chemicals like mercury, cadmium and lead can leak into the ground and cause pollution.

Advantages of rechargeable cells:
- Can be used many times over.
- Less expensive in the long run.
- Fewer cells are discarded into the environment.
- Less of a drain on energy resources.

Disadvantages of rechargeable batteries:
- Need to buy a charger.
- More expensive to buy.
- Contain carcinogenic (cancer-causing) chemicals.
- Can go 'flat' without warning (so unsuitable for smoke detectors, etc.).

Battery Capacity

The **capacity** of a battery is a measure of how much energy it can store and is given in units called **amp-hours** (Ah). 1 amp-hour (Ah) is equal to 1 amp (A) of electric current for 1 hour.

Capacity tells you how long a battery will work for before it goes 'flat' (uses all its stored energy). The higher the amp-hour rating, the more energy is stored in the battery.

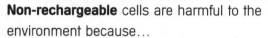

Capacity (Ah) = **Current (A)** X **Hours (h)**

Example

A car battery has a capacity of 40Ah. Calculate the number of hours it can operate for at a current of 1A.

Rearrange the formula

$$\text{Hours} = \frac{\text{Capacity}}{\text{Current}}$$

$$= \frac{40Ah}{1A}$$

$$= \textbf{40 hours}$$

N.B. As a general rule, the heavier a lead acid battery is, the greater its capacity.

Producing and Measuring Electricity

Electromagnetic Induction

You can make electricity by moving a wire (or coil of wire) so that it cuts through a magnetic field (the lines of force). This will induce a voltage between the ends of the wire. This will cause electrons to flow along the wire creating an electric current, if the wire is part of a complete circuit.

The greater the potential difference, the greater the electron flow (or 'drift') and the greater the current.

Voltage, or **potential difference**, is the measure of electrical force. It's measured in **volts** using a **voltmeter**. The voltage induced can be increased by...

- using stronger **magnets**
- using more coils of wire
- moving the wire (or magnet) faster.

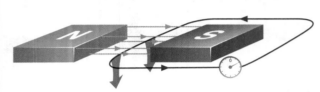

Moving the wire into the magnetic field induces a current in one direction.

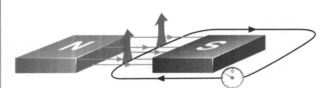

Moving the wire out of the magnetic field induces a current in the opposite direction.

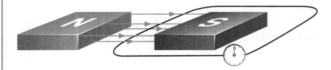

If the wire isn't moved, no current will be induced.

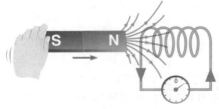

Moving the magnet into the coil induces a current in one direction.

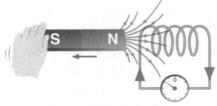

Moving the magnet out of the coil induces a current in the opposite direction.

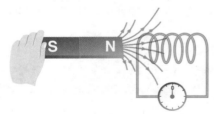

If neither magnet nor coil is moved, no current will be induced.

Generators and Dynamos

Generators use the principle of rotating coils of wire in a magnetic field to generate electricity; a coil of wire cuts through a magnetic field to induce a voltage.

The same effect can be achieved by rotating a magnet within a coil of wire.

Bicycle dynamos use the turning motion of the bicycle's wheels to generate electricity for the bicycle's lights. The size of the electric current is determined by...

- the speed the wheel is turning
- the magnet's strength
- the number of coils of wire.

Resistance

Resistance is a measure of how hard it is for a current to flow through a conductor. Resistance is measured in **ohms** (Ω).

Each part of a circuit tries to resist the flow of electrons (current). Even good conductors, for example, copper wire, have resistance but it's so low it can normally be ignored.

In a **series circuit**, resistance increases as more components are added. For a given fixed voltage, the same current flows through each part of the circuit. The potential difference is $V = V_1 + V_2$.

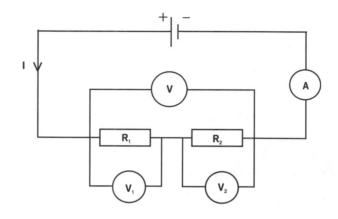

 HT

In a **parallel circuit**, resistance stays the same no matter how many components are added. The potential difference across each of the resistors is the same. For a fixed voltage, the current in the main circuit is $I = I_1 + I_2$.

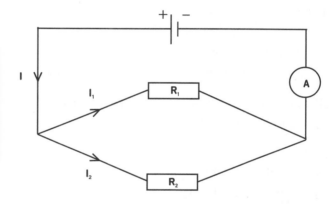

Calculating Resistance

Resistance, voltage and **current** are related by the following formula:

Voltage (volt, V) $=$ Current (ampere, A) $\times$ Resistance (ohm, Ω)

As a greater voltage is supplied to a series circuit, the current increases which makes the bulb(s) brighter.

The greater the resistance, the smaller the current. The larger the voltage, the greater the current.

Examples

1 Find the voltage needed to cause a current of 2A to pass through a conductor of resistance 50Ω.

Voltage = Current x Resistance

    = 2A x 50Ω

    = **100V**

2 A potential difference of 12V is put across a conductor of resistance 24Ω. Find the current that flows through the resistor.

Current = $\dfrac{\text{Voltage}}{\text{Resistance}}$

= $\dfrac{12V}{24\Omega}$ = **0.5A**

3 A potential difference of 24V placed across a conductor causes a current of 0.2A to flow through the conductor. What is the conductor's resistance?

Resistance = $\dfrac{\text{Voltage}}{\text{Current}}$ = $\dfrac{24V}{0.2A}$ = **120Ω**

Key Words

Dynamo • **Magnet** • **Parallel circuit** • **Potential difference** • **Resistance** • **Series circuit** • **Voltage**

Producing and Measuring Electricity

Resistors

A **resistor** is a component that has a fixed resistance.

When an electric current passes through a resistor, the moving electrons collide with atoms within the resistor, giving up their energy.

This results in the temperature of the resistor increasing.

Resistor

Light-Dependent Resistors (LDR)

The resistance of a **light-dependent resistor** (LDR) depends on light intensity. Its resistance decreases as light intensity increases:

* In the dark, resistance is typically 10MΩ (1 000 000 ohms).
* In the sunlight, resistance is typically 100Ω.

LDRs are made from a semiconductor called cadmium sulphide (CdS).

LDRs are used to control the exposure time (how long the shutter is open) of a digital camera – in poor light, the shutter needs to be open for longer.

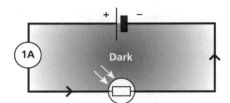

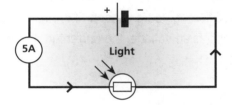

Thermistors

Thermistors are also made from semiconductor materials.

The resistance of a thermistor depends on the surrounding temperature. The higher the temperature, the lower the resistance.

Thermistors are used as electronic thermometers, for example, they're used to control central heating to maintain a constant temperature.

The following electrical appliances use thermistors:

* hairdryers
* immersion heaters
* toasters
* light bulbs
* televisions.

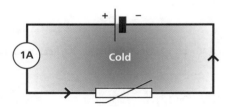

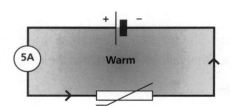

Producing and Measuring Electricity

Current–Voltage Graphs

Current–voltage graphs show how the current through a component varies with the voltage across it. The circuit shows an experiment set-up to investigate the behaviour of an unknown component:

- All components are connected in series.
- The voltmeter is connected in parallel.
- The variable resistor (called a rheostat) allows the current to be adjusted.
- Other components can be investigated using this circuit.

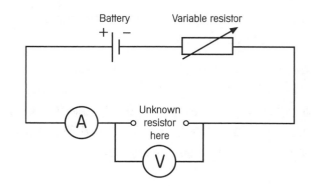

Fixed-Value Resistor

For a component with a fixed value of resistance (R), the results of the experiment are shown in the table.

R (Ω)	Volts (V)	Current (A)
2	2	1
2	3	1.5
2	4	2

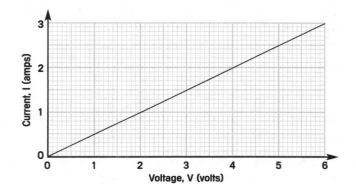

The graph plot shows a straight line through the origin. This means that the current (I) is proportional to the voltage (V), i.e. $V = I \times R$ (known as Ohm's Law).

Filament Lamp

For a component with a variable resistance such as a filament lamp, e.g. torch bulb, the results are shown in the table.

R (Ω)	Volts (V)	Current (A)
2	2	1
2.14	3	1.4
2.22	4	1.8

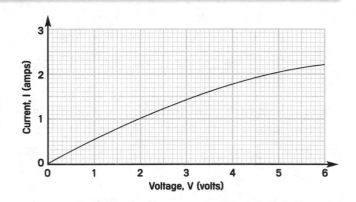

The graph is not a straight line and doesn't obey the rule $V = I \times R$. As more current flows, the metal filament gets hotter and so its resistance **increases**. The line curves and becomes flatter.

Key Words

Light-dependent resistor • Resistor • Thermistor

Producing and Measuring Electricity

Electricity and the Modern World

Electricity has had a huge impact on the making of the modern world.

The electric telephone, invented by Alexander Graham Bell in 1876 used only a small amount of electricity, which could be supplied along the phone line, so mains electricity wasn't required. This marked the beginning of modern electrical communications.

In 1920, only 10% of homes had an electricity supply and most of the household chores were done manually. Now (nearly) every home in developed countries has a supply of mains electricity and there's a vast number of appliances that have been developed that operate using electricity.

This in turn has reduced the amount of time it takes to perform certain tasks, such as washing clothes, which means that people have more free time.

Computer Technology

The invention of the transistor (replacing the valve) and microchip, on which integrated circuits could be built, led to the further development of modern computers.

Digital technology based on 0s and 1s (binary) allowed the development of smaller and smaller switches and microscopic electronic circuits. Modern integrated circuits have millions of transistors compacted into a tiny space. This has led to an increase in the speed of processing, leading to the development of numerous applications.

The following are some possible uses for this new microtechnology:
- Medical monitoring (to constantly display patients' pulse rates, etc.).
- Tiny watches and mobile phones, etc. that can be worn like sticking plasters.

Key Words

Superconductivity

HT Superconductivity

In 1911, Onnes discovered that when materials were cooled to certain temperatures, they had zero resistance, or 'superconductivity'. They were called superconductors.

Zero resistance only occurs at very low temperatures in a few materials, but research is being carried out to achieve superconductivity at higher temperatures.

In 1933, Meissner discovered that superconductors expelled magnetic flux from within them. So, when placed in an external magnetic field, the magnetic fluxes are repelled, and produce large currents that can circulate indefinitely.

These, and other, scientific advances have enabled new technology to be developed. For example, the **Maglev** (magnetic levitation) **train** (proposed in 1934) uses superconductivity. Electrified coils in the walls and track create a magnetic field. The magnetised coil running along the track repels the large electromagnets on the train's undercarriage, allowing it to levitate.

Power is supplied to the coils within the track walls to create magnetic fields that pull / push the train along. This eliminates friction and allows the train to travel at over 500km/h. But, they have proved to be too expensive to be practical.

Producing and Measuring Electricity

Glossary of Key Words

Ammeter – an instrument used to measure electric current.

Ampere-hours / Amp-hours – the electric charge flowing in one hour through a conductor passing one ampere.

Battery – a device that uses a chemical reaction to generate electricity.

Battery capacity – a measure of how much energy a battery is able to store; normally measured in ampere-hours (Ah).

Current – the rate of flow of electrons through a conductor. It's measured in amperes / amps, A, or milliamps, mA.

Dry cell – the most common type of battery; contains no liquid.

Dynamo – a device for generating electricity from the simple rotational motion of a coil in a magnetic field, or the rotation of a magnet inside a coil.

Light-dependent resistor (LDR) – an electronic component whose resistance varies with light intensity.

Magnet – a magnetised piece of metal surrounded by a magnetic field.

Potential difference – the difference in the values of the electrical potentials at two points or the work done in moving unit charge from one to another.

Rechargeable – a battery which is able to have its chemical energy replaced.

Resistance – the property of materials to resist the flow of electric current through them; measured in ohms, Ω.

Resistor – an electronic component designed to produce a known (fixed) resistance.

Series circuit – a circuit in which all the components are connected in one continuous loop, with a common current running through them all.

Solar cell – a device that is able to transform light energy into electrical energy.

Thermistor – an electronic component whose resistance varies with temperature.

Voltage – the value of the potential difference between two points. It's measured in volts, V or millivolts, mV.

HT **Parallel circuit** – a circuit in which each component is connected to the battery by its own loop, with a common current running through them all.

Superconductivity – a property of materials that have no resistance to electric current at low temperatures.

Practice Questions

1 Which of the following supplies give a source of direct current? Tick the correct options.

    A Solar cells   ◯

    B Batteries   ◯

    C Mains electricity   ◯

    D Electrical generators   ◯

2 A zinc–carbon torch battery has a capacity of 2Ah. Calculate the number of hours it can operate for a current of 0.01A.

3 In electromagnetic induction, which of the following methods can be used to increase the voltage? Tick the correct options.

    A Using stronger magnets   ◯

    B Moving the wire (or magnet) slower   ◯

    C Moving the wire (or magnet) faster   ◯

    D Using more coils of wire   ◯

4 **a)** A potential difference of 4V is applied to a resistor. The current flowing through the resistor is 0.04A. Calculate the value of the resistance.

    b) An additional resistance of 50Ω is added in parallel to the circuit. Calculate the current flowing through this resistance.

5 Find the voltage needed across a conductor of resistance 200Ω to cause a current of 0.2A to pass through.

6 Which of the following are applications for thermistors? Tick the correct options.

   A   Aperture control in a digital camera ◯

   B   Protecting filaments in projector lamps ◯

   C   Controlling central heating systems ◯

   D   Controlling light levels ◯

7 Choose the correct word from the options given to complete the following sentence.

the same   **different**   **increased**   **decreased**

For resistances in a series circuit, the potential difference across each component is

_____ .

8 Tick the correct option to complete the following sentence: For a thermistor, the current–voltage relationship shows…

   A   a straight-line (current is proportional to voltage) ◯

   B   an increase in current against voltage ◯

   C   a decrease in current against voltage ◯

   D   no current flows at all voltages ◯

9 Which of the following major developments in electronics was / were a result of the invention of the microchip? Tick the correct options.

   A   Integrated circuits ◯

   B   Mobile phone technology ◯

   C   Microcomputers ◯

   D   Broadband ◯

HT

10 When certain materials are cooled to a very low temperature they have zero resistance. What is the name given to this phenomenon? Tick the correct option.

   A   Superfluidity ◯

   B   Supercritical ◯

   C   Superconductivity ◯

   D   Supercooling ◯

11 Name one application where zero resistance materials have been used.

_____

You're in Charge

Energy Sources

Electricity is a secondary source of energy. There are two types of primary sources of energy that can be used to produce it.

Renewable energy sources, for example, wind, waves and solar energy…
- are sources of energy that will not run out, or that can be replaced
- produce electricity by driving turbines directly
- don't produce pollution
- can have high initial set-up costs
- change the appearance of their surroundings.

Examples of how different renewable energy sources can be used to produce electricity are given below, together with the advantages (+) and disadvantages (-) of each source.

Non-renewable energy sources, for example, coal, oil and gas…
- are energy sources that will eventually run out
- are burned to produce electricity
- produce pollution when they're burned.

Coal is a **non-renewable energy source** that's used to generate electricity in power stations:
1. Coal is burned to heat water.
2. The steam produced is used to drive turbines.
3. The turbines rotate a generator, producing electricity.

Coal is an easily accessible energy source but it produces pollution, spoils the appearance of the landscape and it will eventually run out.

Biomass / Wood

Wood is a **renewable energy source** that can be used to heat water to produce steam to rotate a turbine and generator.

+ Widely available source.
+ More trees can be grown relatively quickly to replace those that are cut down.

- Produces smoke and waste.
- Costly — trees need to be cut and transported as soon as they're cut down, and more trees need to be planted in their place.
- Changes the landscape.
- Burning wood / biomass releases carbon dioxide into the air.

Wind

Wind power is used to turn the blades of a turbine, causing a generator to spin and produce electricity.

+ Doesn't produce waste or pollution.
+ Free energy source.
- Equipment is expensive to install.
- Each turbine has a low output, so lots of turbines are needed.
- Wind is unreliable.
- Causes visual pollution.

Tidal

At high tide, water is trapped by a barrage. At low tide, the water is released back to the same level as the sea. The movement of the released water is used to drive a turbine to generate electricity.

+   Doesn't produce waste or pollution.
+   Free energy source.
+   Reliable energy source.
+   High output – operates almost continuously.
-   Spoils appearance of river.
-   Interferes with river traffic.
-   Damages habitats.

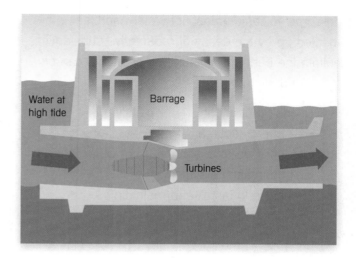

Waves

The motion of the waves makes the nodding duck move up and down. The movement of the nodding duck is translated into a rotary movement, which turns a generator to produce electricity.

+   Doesn't produce waste or pollution.
+   Free energy source.
-   Equipment is expensive to install.
-   Variable wave size means unreliable, low output.
-   Changes appearance of coastline and is a danger to ships.

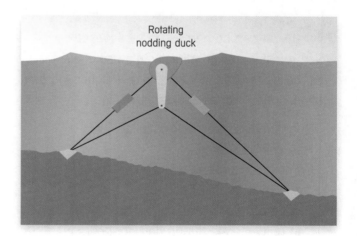

Hydro-Electricity

Water stored in reservoirs above a power station is released and drives turbines as it flows downwards. The water is pumped back up to the higher reservoir when demand is low.

+   Doesn't produce waste or pollution.
+   Reliable and free energy source.
+   Fast response – can support the National Grid during high demand.
+   High output – the water can be re-used.
-   Damages habitats and villages.
-   Requires high rainfall and mountainous area.
-   Changes appearance of surroundings.

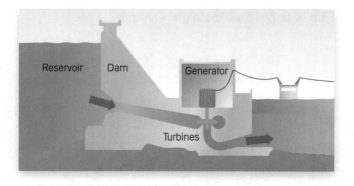

Key Words
Electricity • Wind power

You're in Charge

Geothermal

In some volcanic areas, hot water and steam, heated up by the decay of **radioactive** substances within the Earth, rise naturally. The steam can be used to drive turbines.

+ Doesn't produce waste or pollution.
+ Free energy source.
+ Can be used as a source of hot water when it isn't generating electricity.
- Expensive to install and maintain.
- Few suitable sites.
- Low output.

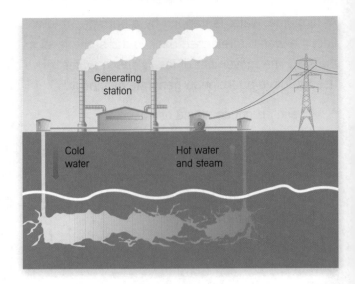

Generating station

Cold water

Hot water and steam

Solar Power

Solar power can be harnessed by **solar cells**, which transfer sunlight directly into useful electricity. Solar cells are used in calculators, watches, garden lighting, space probes and satellites.

+ Don't produce waste or pollution.
+ Free energy source.
+ No need for turbines and generators.
+ Very light and easily portable.
+ Can be used on very small scale, e.g. calculators.
- Can only operate during daylight hours.

A solar cell is generally **less than 20% efficient** (i.e. only about 20% of the captured energy from the Sun is transferred into light energy).

Solar cells are currently used only in sunny or remote places where it's more difficult to get other forms of electrical supply. If the efficiency of solar cells can be increased to enable them to operate effectively with less sunlight, then they could be more useful around the world.

🛈 The Future of Energy

Non-renewable energy sources will eventually run out. They're major **polluters** and contributors to **global warming**. Currently, the **National Grid** collects all the electrical energy generated in power stations and distributes it. But, as more smaller systems (e.g. renewable sources) are used to generate and contribute to the National Grid, a revised distribution system will need to be put in place.

The benefits and drawbacks of new methods of producing electricity need be considered at a national level. People need to change their attitudes towards visual pollution and accept the high set-up costs.

Direct Current Electric Motors

Direct current (DC) **electric** motors can be found in many electrical devices. This is how they work:

1. Current flows through the coil.
2. Each side of the coil creates a magnetic field.
3. The magnetic field interacts with the permanent magnetic field of the magnet.
4. The force created acts on both sides of the coil, causing it to rotate.

Split-Ring Commutator

In order to keep the **coil rotating continuously** in a DC motor, the **current reverses direction** every half turn, using the split-ring **commutator**.

Each end of the coil is connected to one half of the commutator. An electric current flows in through one half of the commutator via the carbon brushes, passes through the coil, then flows out of the other half of the commutator, causing the coil to rotate.	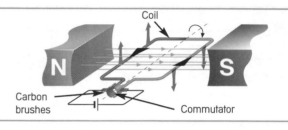
As the coil rotates, it reaches a vertical position. No current flows through it because the commutator no longer makes contact with the brushes (each section of the commutator is separated by an insulator). But, the coil rotates past this vertical position due to its own momentum.	
Each half of the commutator is now connected to the other end of the coil, so the direction of the current through the coil is reversed. The coil continually rotates in the same direction because the current reverses its direction of flow through the coil every half turn.	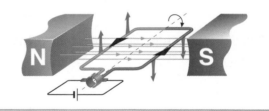

Electrical power

The power of an appliance is determined by the rate at which electrical energy is transferred. This is measured in **joules per second** (J/s) or watts (W).

You can calculate the power of an appliance using the current and voltage:

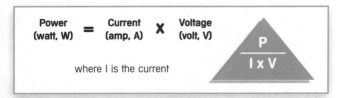

where I is the current

Example

A current of 3.75A runs through an iron at 240V. What is the power of the iron?

Power = Current x Voltage
= 3.75A x 240V = **900W**

Key Words

Energy • Motor • Power • Solar cell • Solar power • Voltage

You're in Charge

Kilowatt-Hours

Energy from the mains supply is measured in **kilowatt-hours (kWh)**, often called a unit. An electrical appliance that transfers 1kWh of energy, transfers 1 kilowatt (1000W) of power for 1 hour.

You can calculate the cost of using an appliance for a specified length of time using this formula:

> **Cost (p) = Power (kW) X Time (h) X Cost of 1kWh (p)**

Example

A 200W television is switched on for 10 hours. What is the cost of the electricity used by the television if 1kWh costs 7p?

Cost = Power x Time x Cost of 1kWh
= 0.2kW x 10 hours x 7p
= **14p**

Efficiency

When devices transfer energy, some of it is **usefully transferred** to where it's wanted and in the form that's wanted. The remainder is '**wasted**'.

The amount of useful energy transferred by an appliance is called the **efficiency** of the appliance. You can calculate the efficiency of an appliance using this formula:

> **Efficiency = $\dfrac{\text{Useful output}}{\text{Total input}}$ X 100%**

N.B. No device can have an efficiency greater than 100%.

The total amount of energy before the transfer is equal to the total amount of energy after the transfer. This is called the **principle of conservation of energy**.

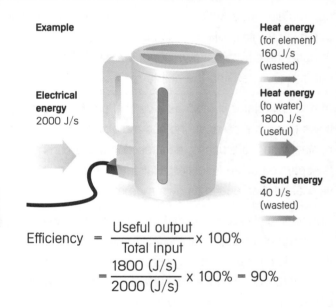

Example

- Electrical energy 2000 J/s
- Heat energy (for element) 160 J/s (wasted)
- Heat energy (to water) 1800 J/s (useful)
- Sound energy 40 J/s (wasted)

Efficiency $= \dfrac{\text{Useful output}}{\text{Total input}} \times 100\%$

$= \dfrac{1800 \ (\text{J/s})}{2000 \ (\text{J/s})} \times 100\% = 90\%$

So 10% of the input energy is wasted, i.e. as heat and sound.

House Insulation

All buildings lose heat in various ways.

Insulating houses means less energy is required to heat them, which means that less of the world's energy resources are used and fuel bills are cheaper.

But, it costs money to install insulation, so in order to compare energy saving measures you can calculate the **payback time**:

> **Payback time = $\dfrac{\text{Installation cost}}{\text{Annual saving}}$**

Key Words

Double insulation • Earth wire • Efficiency • Fuse • Insulation • Residual current circuit breakers

Three-Pin Plug

A three-pin plug contains the following components:

- **Earth wire** (green and yellow)
- **Fuse**
- **Neutral wire** (blue)
- **Live wire** (brown) – carries the current.
- **Cable grip**
- **Casing** – made of an insulator, e.g. plastic or rubber.

The alternating current passes to the connected appliance through the neutral and live wires.

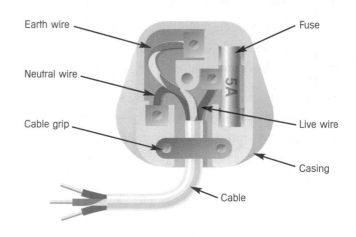

Safety Devices

A **fuse** is a short, thin piece of wire with a low melting point. If the current passing through the appliance exceeds the fuse's rating, the fuse wire gets hot, melts and breaks. This prevents damage to the cable, appliance, and user.

For this safety system to work properly, the current rating of the fuse must be slightly higher than the normal working current of the appliance.

All electrical appliances with outer metal cases must be **earthed**. The earth wire connects the metal outer case of an appliance to the earth pin in the plug.

If a fault in the appliance connects the live wire to the case, the case will become live. The current will 'run to earth' through the earth wire because it offers less resistance. This overload of current will cause the fuse wire to melt.

Some appliances are **double insulated**, which means that all of the metal parts inside the appliance are completely insulated from any outer part of the appliance that may be handled. These appliances don't need an earth wire.

HT Most modern houses have **residual current circuit breakers** (**RCCBs**). A circuit breaker contains an **electromagnet** that **separates** a pair of contacts when it detects a difference between the current running through the live and neutral wires. Each circuit in a house (e.g. downstairs lights) will have its own RCCB.

Advantages of RCCBs (compared to fuses):

- Very safe (don't get hot).
- React more quickly to a fault.
- Easy to reset.
- Easy to see which circuit has a fault.
- Easy to switch off a circuit that needs to be repaired.

You're in Charge

Developing Technologies

Scientific knowledge and understanding have led to the development of new technologies (e.g. in medicine), which have a huge impact on society.

Scientific ideas change and develop over time. The scientific knowledge and technologies that we have today are the products of thousands of years of observation, questioning and investigation. As scientific understanding in one field grows and develops, it often enables growth and development to take place in other related areas of science. The process of developing scientific ideas is summarised in this flow chart.

A phenomenon is observed.

Scientists develop hypotheses or theories based on the observation and current scientific knowledge.

Research and investigations are carried out to test the hypotheses and theories.

The results are analysed and conclusions are drawn.

The hypothesis or theories are changed, refined or discounted.

HT **Electricity and Medicine**

The table outlines how the key discoveries about electricity have aided the development of electrotherapy in medicine.

In the future, our understanding of electricity and its effects on the body will continue to develop and technologies will become safer and more efficient.

Year	Discovery	Result
1745	Electrical capacitor invented.	Static electricity accumulated and studied.
1746	Jean Jallabert discovered muscles could be stimulated using electricity.	Capacitor used to successfully treat a paralysed patient.
1781	Luigi Galvani deduced that muscle contractions were caused by electricity flowing through nerves.	Realisation that electricity could be used in medical treatments.
1804	Charles Wilkinson published guidelines for using electricity to treat certain conditions.	Electricity used to treat certain conditions, e.g. tetanus, tumours and paralysis.
1820–1831	Understanding of electromagnetic induction and development of generators.	Steady supply of electricity for medical use.
1860s	Current induced in induction coil.	Current used to diagnose conditions such as paralysis.
1890s	Jacques d'Arsonval discovered that higher-frequency currents reduced the pain experienced by patients. Heinrich Hertz invented a machine that generated high-frequency currents.	High-frequency currents used to destroy tumours. Treatments became pain-free. Anaesthetic effect of high-frequency currents used to relieve chronic rheumatism, nervous conditions and neuralgic pains.
1970s	Development of TENS (Transcutaneous Electrical Nerve Stimulation).	Pain signals, during childbirth for example, were able to be blocked.
2000	Uses of EMS (Electrical Muscle Stimulation) investigated.	Enabled some paralysed people to regain some sensation and movement.

Glossary of Key Words

Double insulation – wiring that has at least two layers of insulating material around live parts.

Earth wire – a wire that connects an appliance to the earth (ground), normally via a plug and socket.

Efficiency – the ratio of the useful energy obtained from a device compared to the amount of energy put into the device to operate it.

Electricity – electric current used as a source of power.

Energy – the ability to do work. It can't be created or destroyed, i.e. there's a fixed amount, but it can be transferred from place to place, and transformed into different types (e.g. from electrical into light). Measured in Joules, J, or kWh.

Fuse – a device containing a thin piece of wire that protects appliances by melting (to put a gap in a circuit) if the current becomes too high.

Insulation – reduces the transfer of heat energy.

Motor – a device used to produce kinetic energy from a power source, normally as the result of a current flowing around a coil in a magnetic field.

Power – the rate at which work is done, or energy is transferred, by a device. Measured in watts, W, or kilowatts, kW.

Solar cell – a device that converts light energy directly into electrical energy.

Solar power – the power from the Sun's radiation.

Voltage – the value of the potential difference between two points, e.g. the two terminals of a cell; measured in volts, V, or millivolts, mV.

Wind power – power produced from the motion of the wind, e.g. by a wind turbine.

(HT) **Residual Current Circuit Breakers** (**RCCB**) - an electrical device that disconnects a circuit whenever it detects a difference between the current in the live and neutral wires.

Practice Questions

1. Which of the following energy sources are renewable energy sources? Tick the correct options.

   A Coal ⬭   **B** Biomass / wood ⬭

   C Wind ⬭   **D** Natural gas ⬭

2. Which of the following statements are advantages of a hydro-electric power station? Tick the correct options.

   A High output (the water can be reused) ⬭   **B** Damages habitats ⬭

   C Doesn't produce waste or pollution ⬭   **D** Expensive to install ⬭

3. Choose the correct words from the options given to complete the following sentences.

watches	sunlight	solar cells	calculators	electricity

   a) Solar power can be harnessed by _____, which transfer _____

   directly into useful _____ .

   b) They are used in _____ , space probes, _____ and satellites.

4. What are the two functions of a split-ring commutator?

   a) _____   b) _____

5. Give an example of a power supply that supplies the following:

   a) a direct current _____

   b) an alternating current _____

6. Choose the correct words from the options given to complete the following sentences.

power	efficiency	watts	electrical	percentage	decimal	Newtons

   a) The proportion of useful energy transferred by an electrical appliance is called the

   _____ of the appliance. It is given as a _____ .

   b) The _____ of an appliance is determined by the rate at which

   _____ energy is transferred. It is measured in joules per second, or

   _____ .

7 A 2000W shower is switched on for 12 minutes. What is the cost of the electricity used by the shower if 1kWh costs 8p? Give your answer to the nearest penny.

8 Which of the following are parts of a three-pin plug? Tick the correct options.

    A Live wire ◻

    B Residual current circuit breaker ◻

    C Neutral wire ◻

    D Insulated casing ◻

9 All electrical appliances with outer metal cases must be 'earthed'. What does this statement mean?

HT

10 Write **advantage** or **disadvantage** next to each of the following statements about RCCBs.

    a) React quickly to a fault.

    b) Costly to install.

    c) Easy to reset after a fault.

    d) Very safe (don't get hot).

11 The following statements describe the process of developing scientific ideas. Put the statements in the correct order by writing the numbers **1–5** in the boxes.

    A Results are analysed ◻

    B Hypotheses or theories are developed ◻

    C Phenomenon is observed ◻

    D Research is performed to test hypotheses and theories ◻

    E Hypotheses or theories are changed, refined, or discounted ◻

Now You See It, Now You Don't

Waves

Waves transfer energy from one point to another without transferring any matter. They have the following features:

- **Amplitude** – the maximum vertical disturbance caused by a wave (i.e. its height).
- **Wavelength** – the distance between corresponding points on two successive disturbances.
- **Frequency** – the number of waves produced (or that pass a particular point) in one second.

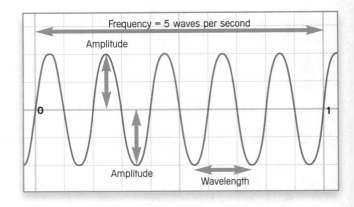

Types of Waves

Transverse waves, e.g. all electromagnetic waves (light, infrared, etc.)…

- carry energy
- have a pattern of disturbance that's at right angles (90°) to the direction of movement
- can travel across a **vacuum**, i.e. don't need a medium.

Longitudinal waves, e.g. sound, ultrasound and seismic waves…

- carry energy
- have a pattern of disturbance that's in the same direction as the direction of wave movement
- can only travel through a medium.

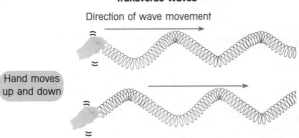

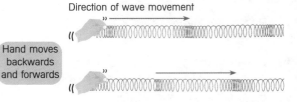

Wave Speed

You can calculate **wave speed** using this formula:

> **Wave speed (m/s) = Frequency (Hz) X Wavelength (m)**

Example

A sound wave has a frequency of 168Hz and a wavelength of 2m. What is the speed of the wave?

Wave speed = Frequency x Wavelength
$$= 168\text{Hz} \times 2\text{m} = \textbf{336m/s}$$

You can calculate speed using this formula:

> $$\text{Speed (m/s)} = \frac{\text{Distance (m)}}{\text{Time taken (s)}}$$

Example

In echo sounding, ultrasonic waves are sent out from the bottom of a ship to the bottom of the sea. The length of time it takes to receive the reflected rays can be used to calculate the depth of the water. In one test, a sound wave takes 0.5s to travel from the transmitter to the receiver. The speed of sound in water is 1400m/s. How deep is the sea?

Distance = Speed x Time
$$= 1400 \times 0.5 = 700\text{m}$$

Depth of sea $= \dfrac{700}{2} = \textbf{350m}$

Rearrange the formula

This is the total distance travelled by the wave to the seabed, and back again, so you need to divide this answer by 2

Now You See It, Now You Don't

Electromagnetic Waves

The **electromagnetic spectrum** is made up of waves that have different frequencies and wavelengths.

All the waves in the electromagnetic spectrum...
- carry energy
- are transverse
- travel at the speed of light in a vacuum
- travel through a vacuum at the same speed.

To help you remember the waves in the electromagnetic spectrum in order of increasing wavelength, use this mnemonic: **G**ood **X**ylophones **U**se **V**ery **I**nteresting **M**usical **R**hythms.

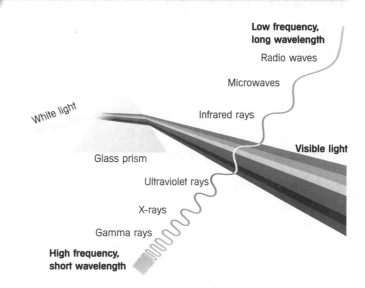

Dangers of Waves

X-rays and **gamma rays** are used in medicine. They can both pass through soft tissues, although some rays are **absorbed**:
- Low doses can cause cancer, through the destruction or **mutation** of cells.
- High doses can kill normal cells.

Infrared rays are used in remote controls, grills and toasters. They are absorbed by the skin and can be felt as heat. Too much exposure to infrared rays will cause burns.

Ultraviolet (UV) rays are used in sunbeds. There are three types of UV **radiation**:
- **UVA** passes through glass, penetrates deep into the skin, and causes early ageing, wrinkles, DNA damage, cancer and some sunburn.
- **UVB** is mostly absorbed by the ozone layer and the atmosphere. Dangers are the same as for UVA, but it also stimulates the production of essential vitamin D.
- **UVC** is the most damaging. But it's mostly absorbed by the ozone layer and the atmosphere.

Low amplitude UV is absorbed by the Earth's atmosphere. We are at most risk from UVB as almost all UVC is absorbed by the ozone layer.

UV rays pass through the skin into the tissues. Darker skin allows less penetration and, therefore, more protection.

High doses of UV rays can kill normal cells and lower doses can cause skin cancer.

The higher the frequency of the wave and the shorter the wavelength, the greater damage it causes.

Waves that have a greater amplitude carry more energy, which means the wave is more likely to be dangerous.

HT The higher the frequency of the waves, the greater the energy of the wave. Gamma rays have the highest frequency and radio waves have the lowest frequency.

Key Words

Absorption • Amplitude • Electromagnetic spectrum • Frequency • Gamma rays • Infrared • Longitudinal • Mutation • Radiation • Transverse • Ultraviolet • Vacuum • Wavelength • Wave • X-rays

Now You See It, Now You Don't

Microwaves

Microwaves are used in communication devices, e.g. in mobile phones. They can be dangerous because...

- they can be absorbed by the water in the cells in your body, causing internal heating of body tissue which may damage or kill cells
- they can produce magnetic fields, which can affect how our cells work.

Mobile phones and masts give out microwave radiation:

- Phones radiate up to 0.25W.
- Masts radiate up to 100W.

Some people claim that the radiation **emitted** by mobile phones and masts poses a health risk.

They claim that microwaves interfere with electrical signals in the body, causing headaches, dizziness and even cancer. But there isn't any strong scientific evidence to support this.

Exposure to microwave radiation from a mast when standing underneath it is less than from a phone. When you are close to a mast, the phone sends a weaker signal. This means less energy is needed so less radiation will penetrate your head.

Therefore, living in remote areas away from a mast could, theoretically, be more dangerous to mobile users, than living close to a mast.

HT Waves in Society

Much of today's technology is based on waves, for example, mobile phones. While mobile phones have many benefits, some studies appear to indicate that their use could be linked with brain tumours and cancer.

Mobile phones do warm the brain slightly but it isn't by as much as would result from vigorous exercise. Because mobile phones are a recent innovation, there haven't been any long-term studies on the possible effects they could have on our health.

Benefits:

- Convenient method of communication.
- Make it easy to keep in touch with people.
- Can help in solving crime because they can be tracked.

Problems:

- It's too early to be certain of the effects because health problems can take time to develop.
- Some people may be at higher risk of health problems due to genetic factors.
- Children may be more vulnerable because their nervous system is still developing and they have a thinner skull, so more energy might be absorbed in the tissues in the brain.

Key Words

Emission • Fluorescent • Microwave • Reflection • Scanning • Ultrasound

Now You See It, Now You Don't

Scanning by Absorption

X-rays can be used to see **bone fractures**:

1. The area with the fracture is placed in front of a photographic plate and is exposed to X-rays.
2. The X-rays are absorbed by the bone but they pass through the fracture.
3. An image is created that clearly shows where any fractures are.

Microwaves are absorbed by water molecules. So, satellites can produce pictures of **weather patterns**.

When different papers and inks are exposed to **UV light**, they absorb, and so emit, different amounts of visible light, which causes them to **fluoresce** differently. This property can be used to **detect forged bank notes**.

Scanning by Emission

The amount of infrared radiation emitted by an object is determined by the temperature: higher temperatures emit more infrared radiation. **Infrared sensors** can detect differences in surface temperature.

This has many uses:
- Police helicopters use infrared sensors to track suspects at night, or in hiding.
- Rescuers use infrared radiation to locate people trapped in collapsed buildings.

Scanning by Reflection

Type of Wave	Uses	Advantages	Disadvantages
Ultrasound (Medical Use)	Used to **scan** pregnant women's abdomens and to detect abnormalities in the body. A scanner sends ultrasonic waves into the body. The waves are partly reflected at any surfaces or boundaries within the body that have a different density or structure, enabling an internal image of the patient to be created.	• Clear examination of soft tissue. • No known harmful effects. • Real-time imaging. • Cost effective.	• Can't penetrate the bone. • Clarity of image is poor. • Requires coupling medium to get rid of air pockets.
Ultrasound (Sonar)	Used in the military, industry and fisheries. An ultrasound pulse is generated and **reflects** from an object in its path as an echo. The time taken to receive the echo gives a measure of how far away the object is.	• Real-time imaging. • Cost effective. • Many applications.	• Clarity of images can be poor. • Accuracy depends on temperature and salt content of the water.
Visible light	Used to recognise an iris (in the eye) or fingerprints. Each iris or fingerprint has its own unique patterns. When the iris or fingerprint is scanned with a low-intensity light, the patterns from the reflected light can be compared with stored images.	• Accurate and secure system.	• Difficult to observe under direct bright light.

Now You See It, Now You Don't

Refraction and Reflection

When a ray of visible or infrared light travels from a medium such as glass, Perspex or water into air, its course changes depending on the angle of incidence:

1. If the ray is **refracted** along the glass–air boundary, the angle of refraction is 90° to the normal and the angle of incidence is known as the **critical angle**.
2. If the angle of incidence is less than the critical angle, the ray is refracted away from the normal. Some rays are also **reflected** from the boundary.
3. If the angle of incidence is greater than the critical angle, no light is refracted; all the light is reflected at the boundary. This is known as **total internal reflection**.

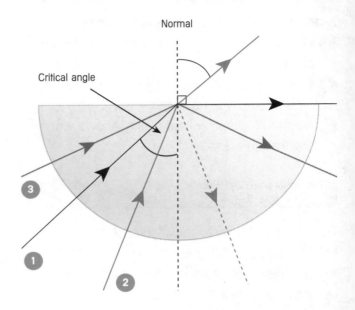

Light and Materials

The speed of an electromagnetic wave, for example, light, depends on the **density** of the material it's travelling through.

The density of a material is its ability to absorb the energy of an electromagnetic wave. The more dense a material is, the slower a wave will move through the material.

The density of the material will influence the critical angle.

Material	Critical Angle with Air (°)	Density (kg/m³)
Ice	50	920
Water	49	1 000
Perspex	42	1 190
Crown Glass	41	2 600
Diamond	24	3 500

Optical Fibres

Optical fibres can be used to transmit large amounts of information over great distances at high speed. The information is carried by a light wave through an optical fibre, which is a long, flexible, transparent cable of very small diameter.

The light is totally internally reflected along the length of the fibre, staying inside it until it emerges at the other end.

Advantages of optical fibres over conventional electrical cables:

- They are thinner, lighter, and are easier to transport.
- They take up less space and many cables can be contained within one protective sleeve.
- They carry more signals.
- They aren't affected by electrical interference.
- They can't be 'tapped'.
- Less frequency amplification is needed.

Now You See It, Now You Don't

Analogue and Digital Signals

Analogue signals vary continuously in amplitude and / or frequency.

Your voice is an analogue signal because it is a sound wave with many different levels of loudness (amplitude) and pitch (frequency).

Digital signals don't vary. The amplitude is sampled (measured) at regular intervals (fractions of a second).

These sampled measurements are then turned into a digital code made up of 0s and 1s, called **binary**.

Analogue Signals

Digital Signals

Advantages of Using Digital Signals

Advantages of using digital signals:
- Several signals can be sent along the same cable at the same time.
- There is no loss in quality: the sequence of 0s and 1s will not change. (Analogue signals lose quality.)
- They can be handled by microprocessors (as in computers).

- More information can be transmitted per second.
- There's no change in the signal information during transmission. If noise (interference) is added during transmission, a regenerator restores the pulses. (Analogue signals can't be cleaned up: if they're amplified the interference is amplified too.)

Digital Technology

Digital technology has had a huge impact on the music industry, which in turn has had a huge impact on the ways in which music can be listened to and distributed:
- Music keyboards can be connected to computers.
- Instruments can be synthesised.
- Tracks can be recorded onto CDs and DVDs, which can hold much more information and have a much higher sound quality than vinyl records, cassettes and videotapes.
- Music can be uploaded to, and downloaded from, the Internet and shared much more easily.
- Music can be compressed (so less storage space is required) and played on MP3 players.
- Radio programmes can be broadcast digitally on DAB (digital audio broadcasting).

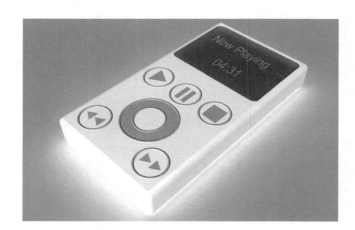

Key Words
Analogue • Digital • Optical fibres • Refraction

Now You See It, Now You Don't

HT Seismic Waves

When an earthquake occurs, two types of seismic wave are generated:

- primary waves (P waves)
- secondary waves (S waves).

Primary waves occur first. They're longitudinal waves, i.e. the ground vibrates up and down. They can travel through solids and liquids.

Secondary waves occur second because they move more slowly. They are transverse waves, i.e. the ground vibrates from left to right. They can't travel through liquids.

Secondary waves (S waves)

Primary waves (P waves)

The Structure of the Earth

Studying seismic waves has provided evidence of the Earth's layered structure. Primary waves are able to reach the opposite side of the Earth; secondary waves don't. This provides evidence that the outer core is liquid.

The Earth has…

- a thin crust
- a mantle which is semi-fluid and extends almost halfway to its centre
- a core, which is over half of its diameter, that has a liquid outer part and a solid inner part.

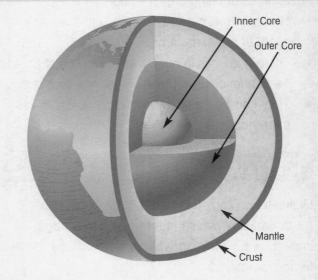

Inner Core

Outer Core

Mantle

Crust

Predicting Earthquakes and Tsunamis

An **earthquake** is caused by the sudden movement of tectonic plates. A **tsunami**, or tidal wave, is caused by an underwater disturbance, normally an earthquake or volcano.

Scientists can only predict where earthquakes will happen, but not when they will happen. They know where the faults in the Earth's crust are, but not how regularly the Earth's tectonic plates move.

Although we aren't able to predict individual earthquakes, the world's largest earthquakes do have a spatial pattern, and estimates of the locations and magnitudes of some future large earthquakes can now be made.

Key Words

Seismic wave

Now You See It, Now You Don't

Glossary of Key Words

Absorption – a substance's ability to absorb energy, e.g. UV into the skin.

Amplitude – the maximum vertical disturbance caused by a wave.

Analogue – a signal that varies continuously in amplitude and / or frequency.

Digital – a signal that uses a binary code (0s and 1s) to represent information.

Electromagnetic spectrum – a continuous arrangement that displays electromagnetic waves in order of increasing frequency or wavelength.

Emission – the outflow of electromagnetic radiation from a system.

Fluorescent – the emission of light by a substance that has been exposed to electromagnetic radiation.

Frequency – the number of complete wave oscillations per second, or the number of complete waves to pass a point in 1 second. Measured in hertz (Hz).

Gamma rays – high-frequency electromagnetic waves with a short wavelength that can damage and kill cells.

Infrared – a region of the electromagnetic spectrum just below the red end of the visible spectrum.

Longitudinal – an energy-carrying wave in which the movement of the particles is in line with the direction in which the energy is being transferred.

Microwave – a type of electromagnetic wave used to carry communication signals.

Mutation – a change in the genetic material of a cell (or virus).

Optical fibres – very thin strands of pure optical glass or plastic that use totally internally reflected light to carry information.

Radiation – the process of transferring energy by electromagnetic waves.

Reflection – the deflection of a ray of light when it hits the boundary between two different materials, e.g. air and glass.

Refraction – the change in direction of a light wave when it passes from one material into another, causing a change in speed (unless the wave hits the second material at a right angle).

Scanning – the act of moving across a surface and applying the same experimental technique at each point, e.g. scanning the intensities of parts of a visual image, for example, in iris recognition.

Transverse – a wave in which the oscillations (vibrations) are at 90° to the direction of energy transfer.

Ultrasound – sound waves that have a frequency above the upper limit of human hearing, i.e. above 20 000Hz.

Ultraviolet – a type of electromagnetic wave, between X-rays and visible light on the spectrum.

Vacuum – a volume of space that contains no particles.

Wave – a moving disturbance that carries energy.

Wavelength – the distance between two corresponding points on successive waves, i.e. the distance between two successive peaks.

X-rays – a region of the electromagnetic spectrum between gamma rays and ultraviolet rays.

(HT) **Seismic wave** – a wave that travels through the Earth, for example, an earthquake.

Practice Questions

1 The diagram shows a wave.

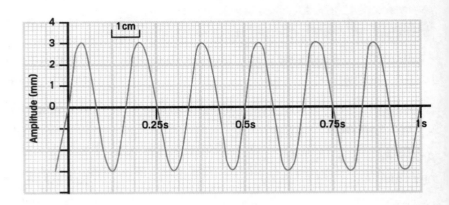

What is its...

a) amplitude (in mm)? ....

b) wavelength (in m)? ....

c) frequency (in Hz)? ....

d) wave speed (in m/s)? ....

....

....

2 What type of wave – **transverse** or **longitudinal** – is each of the following?

a) Infrared wave ....

b) Ultrasound wave ....

c) Sound wave ....

d) Electromagnetic wave ....

3 Which of the following statements about electromagnetic waves are true? Tick the **three** correct options.

    A   UVA radiation is the most damaging of all UV rays   ◯

    B   The higher the frequency, the greater the damage it causes   ◯

    C   Exposure to infrared rays can cause burns   ◯

    D   All waves in the electromagnetic spectrum are transverse   ◯

4 Which of the following statements about mobile phones are true? Tick the correct options.

    A   They give out microwave radiation   ◯

    B   They can cause headaches and dizziness   ◯

    C   They radiate up to 0.25W of radiation   ◯

    D   They produce magnetic fields   ◯

5 Choose the correct words from the options given to complete the sentences.

light   **density**   **refract**   **internal**   **reflected**   **sound**   **mass**

a) Ultrasonic waves are _____ waves.

b) They can be _____ at surfaces or boundaries within the body that have a

different _____ .

c) They can be used to create an _____ image of a patient.

6 Draw lines between the boxes to match each description to the correct term.

Angle of incidence is less than the critical angle		Total internal reflection

Angle of incidence is greater than the critical angle		Refraction

7 Which of the following statements about the advantages of optical fibres over conventional cabling are true? Tick the correct options.

A They aren't affected by electrical interference ⬭

B Many cables are needed, so they take up more space ⬭

C There's less need for regular amplification ⬭

D They can't be 'tapped' ⬭

8 Write **analogue** or **digital** next to each of the following statements about signals.

a) Sound waves _____

b) Signals made from binary code _____

c) Suffer from interference _____

d) No loss of quality _____

HT

9 Which of the following describe a secondary seismic wave? Tick the correct options.

A They can travel through solids ⬭   **B** They can travel through liquids ⬭

C They are transverse ⬭   **D** They are longitudinal ⬭

Space and its Mysteries

The Universe and Our Solar System

The **Universe** is made up of many millions and millions of **galaxies**. Our galaxy is called the Milky Way, which is made up of many millions of **stars**. One particular star in the Milky Way, the Sun, is at the centre of our Solar System.

The **Solar System** is made up of the following:
- the **Sun**
- nine **planets**
- other objects such as moons, **comets** and **asteroids**.

The planets move around the Sun in paths called **orbits**, which are slightly elliptical (squashed circles). Our Moon orbits the Earth at a distance of 380 000km. Stars emit light, whereas planets can only reflect light.

The Hubble Space Telescope has been used to provide detailed images of stars and galaxies.

Planet	Diameter (km)	Distance from Sun (million km)
Mercury	4880	58
Venus	12 112	107.5
Earth	12 742	149.6
Mars	6790	228
Jupiter	142 600	778
Saturn	120 200	1427
Uranus	49 000	2870
Neptune	50 000	4497
Pluto*	2284	5900

*Pluto is now classed as a 'dwarf planet'.

Sun — Mercury — Venus — Earth — Mars — Jupiter — Saturn — Uranus — Neptune — Pluto*
Not to scale

Comets and Asteroids

Comets have a core of frozen gas and dust. They have highly elliptical (very squashed circles) orbits around the Sun. As they approach the Sun, gases evaporate, forming a tail.

Asteroids are rock debris, usually found in a band between the orbits of Mars and Jupiter. Many small asteroids collide with the Earth each year, but they don't usually have much effect.

If a large asteroid or comet were to hit the Earth, the effects could be catastrophic:
- The impact could release tonnes of dust, which would form a layer in the atmosphere and prevent light and heat from reaching the Earth.
- Plants and animals would die due to lack of light and the very low temperature.
- The impact could create tidal waves, which could wipe out settlements on the coast.

The chance of a catastrophic collision is very small, but a comet with a frozen core, which is a few kilometres across is predicted to hit the Earth within the next million years.

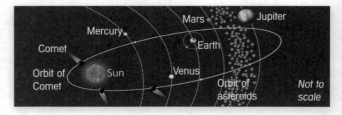

Life of a Star (Stellar Evolution)

Stars don't last forever. Some of the stars you can see in the sky at night will no longer exist. (This is because it takes 4.3 years for the light from the closest star to reach Earth; it can take thousands of years for light from the more distant stars.) The stars are all at different stages in their life cycle.

The life cycle of a star (**stellar** evolution) is as follows:
- **Nebula** (clouds of gases and dust) are pulled together, or collapsed, by gravitational forces.
- The temperature increases as the density increases and nuclear reactions start to take place.
- The reactions, which use hydrogen, release massive amounts of energy and a star is formed.
- Eventually the hydrogen runs out. The star expands and gets colder. What happens next depends upon the size of the star.

These are the stages for a star the size of the Sun (a small-to-average sized star):
1. It becomes a **red giant**.
2. It continues to cool before collapsing under its own gravity to become a **white dwarf**, then a **black dwarf**.

These are the stages for a star much bigger than the Sun:
1. It becomes a **red supergiant**.
2. It shrinks rapidly and explodes (a **supernova**), releasing massive amounts of energy, dust and gas into space.
3. The dust and gas (**nebula**) form new stars and the remains of the supernova will be either a **neutron star** or a **black hole**, depending on the size of the star.

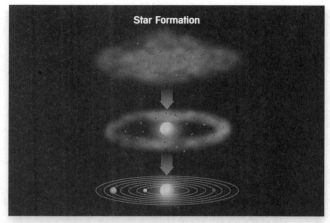

Star Formation

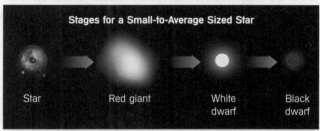

Stages for a Small-to-Average Sized Star

Star — Red giant — White dwarf — Black dwarf

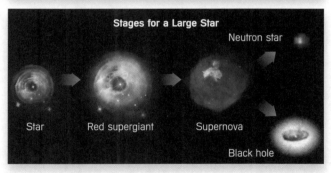

Stages for a Large Star

Star — Red supergiant — Supernova — Neutron star / Black hole

Key Words

Asteroid • Black hole • Comet • Galaxy • Nebula • Orbit • Planet • Star • Stellar • Sun • Universe

ⓗⓣ Black Holes

Black holes are the smallest and most dense known objects. To escape from the gravity of a black hole you need to travel faster than the speed of light. So, anything that approaches a black hole will be pulled in by the huge gravitational pull.

Black holes even bend light that passes close enough to be influenced by its gravitational field. This has an impact on astronomy because light from distant stars and galaxies may have been bent, giving false information on where they actually are.

Space and its Mysteries

Atmosphere and Temperature

In **interplanetary** space there's **no air**, so there's no **atmosphere**.

The **temperature** depends on the distance from the Sun:

- At the Earth's distance, it's about 7°C. (The Earth is, on average, warmer than this because the atmosphere holds the heat in.)
- A thermometer shielded from all the Sun's **radiation** would read about −270°C (nearly absolute zero).

Key Words

Action • Atmosphere • Gravitational field • Gravity • Interplanetary • Radiation • Reaction • Temperature • Weightlessness

Gravity and Radiation

The lack of **gravity** causes astronauts' body fluid to be redistributed: there's less in the legs and more in the face. Scientists have designed special trousers that have air pumped into them to fit tightly, to help keep fluid in the legs.

The heart doesn't need to work as hard in space because it doesn't need to work against gravity. This can cause astronauts to have heart attacks when they return to Earth. Astronauts' bones are also likely to deteriorate in space. To reduce these risks, astronauts must exercise daily.

The Sun emits a lot of harmful **radiation**, especially during solar storms. People on Earth are protected by the Earth's atmosphere and magnetic field.

Astronauts wear white reflective suits to protect them from harmful radiation. Spacecraft are also designed to reflect radiation:

- Water is an effective shield, so scientists are looking at the possibility of surrounding spacecrafts with water tanks.
- Electrostatic fields may also be used.

HT Compensating for Space Conditions

Scientists are trying to find ways to overcome the problems of reduced gravity and radiation from the Sun on long space flights:

- The lack of gravity means that the muscles in the body don't need to work as hard as they do on Earth. To reduce muscle wastage, astronauts must exercise for at least two hours a day on special exercise machines on board the spacecrafts.
- To overcome the weightlessness problems, scientists are working on creating **artificial gravity** by spinning the spacecraft.
- Astronauts need to have with them all the oxygen they require for the journey. Oxygen is needed for breathing and a regular supply is needed at all times. Liquid oxygen is currently used for this supply, but, in the future, plants could be used as an oxygen source (due to photosynthesis).
- The spacecraft rolls constantly to ensure it is evenly exposed to the Sun and has an internal temperature that's habitable by the astronauts (not too hot or cold). If it didn't roll, one side (facing the Sun) would become very hot, whilst the shaded side would be very cold. Unequal exposure to the Sun could crack wires and pipes and any liquid on the cold side would freeze.

Space and its Mysteries

Gravity and the Earth

The Earth and the other planets are held in their orbit around the Sun by gravity. The Earth's gravity keeps the Moon orbiting around the Earth. Earth has sufficient gravity to hold you firmly to its surface and to hold individual gas particles in place, which is why it has an atmosphere.

Space begins where the Earth's atmosphere ends: 100km from the Earth's surface. At this distance, the atmosphere is very thin. The effect of the Earth's gravity doesn't end at 100km. An astronaut's weight will only have fallen by 3% at 100km from the Earth. Even at an altitude of 2600km, gravity is still 50% of its value on Earth.

Weightlessness

The **gravitational force** in interplanetary space is zero: this is why astronauts experience **weightlessness**. When astronauts travel to the Moon they leave the Earth's **gravitational field**, but they're influenced by the Moon's weaker gravitational field. Astronauts become weightless as they move away from the Earth.

Astronauts in spacecraft that orbit the Earth aren't weightless because they're still under the influence of the Earth's gravity. But they do experience weightlessness. The circular motion produces a centripetal force that matches the inward pull of gravity so that the spacecraft is effectively in free fall – just like a free fall parachutist.

Spacecraft: Action and Reaction

In terms of forces, every **action** has an equal and opposite **reaction**: if you push against something and it doesn't move, it means that it pushes back with an equal and opposite force. If the forces don't balance, there will be motion in the direction of the largest force.

Spacecraft engines rely on this principle; the engines burn chemical fuel and the escaping exhaust gases (action force) pushes the spacecraft in the opposite direction (reaction force).

Spacecraft carry their own fuel supply that allows them to go outside the Earth's atmosphere. To achieve this, the engines need to produce enough force to overcome the pull of gravity.

When a spacecraft enters space, there's less gravity so less force is needed to propel the spacecraft. If the spacecraft runs out of reaction mass (fuel) it can't manoeuvre.

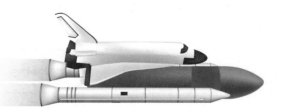

Space and its Mysteries

Gravitational Field Strength

Mass is a measure of how much material there is in an object. The units are grams (g) or kilograms (kg).

Weight is a measure of the force exerted on a mass due to the pull of gravity. The unit is Newtons (N).

Gravitational field strength is measured in Newtons per kilogram (N/kg). On Earth, the gravitational field strength is 10N/kg. On the Moon it's 1.67N/kg (the Moon is a quarter of the diameter of the Earth, 3480km).

The weight of a mass in different gravitational fields can be calculated using the following equation:

> **Weight (N)** = **Mass (kg)** **X** **Gravitational field strength (N/kg)**

If you went to the Moon, your mass would be the same as it is on Earth, but your weight would be less (due to a smaller gravitational force).

Example
An object has a mass of 7kg.

a) Calculate the weight of the object on Earth.

Weight on Earth = Mass x Gravitational field strength

= 7kg x 10N/kg = **70N**

b) Calculate the weight of the object on the Moon.

Weight on Moon = Mass x Gravitational field strength

= 7kg x 1.67N/kg = **11.69N**

Acceleration of Free-Fall

Acceleration of free-fall refers to the greatest acceleration that a mass can achieve when it falls in a gravitational field. It's measured in metres per second per second (m/s^2).

Acceleration of free-fall has the same value as gravitational field strength – it just uses different units.

This means it can also be used as a value for g in the equation for calculating weight:

> **Weight (N)** = **Mass (kg)** **X** **Acceleration of free-fall (m/s^2)**

Force, Mass and Acceleration

Force, mass and acceleration are related by the following equation:

> **Force (N)** = **Mass (kg)** **X** **Acceleration (m/s^2)**

Example
A toy car of mass 800g is accelerated by a force of 0.4N. What is the rate of acceleration?

$$\text{Acceleration} = \frac{\text{Force}}{\text{Mass}}$$

$$= \frac{0.4N}{0.8kg} = \textbf{0.5m/s}^2$$

Extraterrestrial Life

The position of a planet within its solar system determines its potential for the existence of life. A planet should be within a 'habitable zone' orbiting its star (i.e. a similar distance as the Earth is from the Sun).

It's unlikely that our two nearest neighbours (Venus and Mars) will have any life forms. For example, Venus is too hot (its dense atmosphere gives a huge greenhouse effect) and its atmosphere would crush most life forms.

Within our Solar System, some of the larger moons seem more likely to have life forms than the planets. For example…

- **Titan** (Saturn's moon) has a significant atmosphere of organic-rich nitrogen, low gravity, ice and an ocean of liquid ethane.
- **Europa** (Jupiter's moon) is covered with ice and probably has water and a rocky core underneath. It also has sufficient gravity.
- **Triton** (Neptune's moon) has an atmosphere and is covered with an ocean of liquid nitrogen.

Although it's possible that there are basic life forms (e.g. microorganisms) on some moons in the Solar System, we need to find other solar systems to search for intelligent life.

(HT) Evidence **for** the existence of extraterrestrial life:
- There have been many reported sightings.
- Other life forms may not require the same conditions as life on Earth.
- The Universe is so big that there are bound to be many solar systems still undiscovered.

Evidence **against** the existence of extraterrestrial life:
- Earth is unique, so life is unique.
- No other known planet has the same conditions as Earth.
- Searches have never detected anything definite.
- Sightings have never been proven.

Key Words

Acceleration • Mass • Weight

(HT) Life on Other Planets

A star must pass five tests before its planets can be classed as potential homes to extraterrestrial life.

1. It must be on the **main sequence** – the stable state in which stars fuse hydrogen into helium, generating light and heat. Stars stay on the main sequence for a long time, which gives life the chance to evolve.
2. It needs to be in the **right temperature** range. The hottest stars burn out and die quickly, while cooler stars might not produce enough energy to sustain life.
3. It must demonstrate **stable conditions**, otherwise it could alternately freeze or burn any life that develops around it.
4. It must be the **right age**. The Sun is 4.6 billion years old, so life on Earth has had time to develop. The star Alpha Centauri A is older than the Sun, so life may have evolved on its planets.
5. It must have enough of the **heavy elements** (e.g. carbon, nitrogen, oxygen and iron) needed for biological life.

Space and its Mysteries

SETI

Between 1990 and 2005, 130 stars with orbiting planets were found, and the first image of these planets was produced in 2004.

In 1992, NASA set up the Search for **Extraterrestrial** Intelligence **SETI**, which looks for radio signals that may have been emitted by aliens. Using SETI@home, over 50 000 people around the world are helping to process data.

There are two ways of looking for intelligent life in the Universe:

1. Send spaceships out to collect and return data. The main problems with this are the enormous distances and journey times involved — it could take thousands of years.

2. Search for radio signals. Radio telescopes receive information all the time. They are better than light-collecting telescopes at looking for alien signals as light can be blocked by dust particles and gas.

Unmanned Space Exploration

The distances involved in exploring the Solar System, let alone exploring into the Milky Way, are huge. It would take several years for a spacecraft to travel to Pluto. It's not realistic to send manned spacecraft on such long journeys, so data logging and remote sensing is required where information can be sent to receivers on Earth via radio waves.

Unmanned crafts are often used in space exploration because…

- they're safer
- the journey is so long
- the equipment is equally as effective (or more so) than humans (e.g. collecting soil / rock from the surface of a planet or moon, and performing an analysis).

Examples of unmanned spacecraft:

- **Viking Lander** (1975) took images of the surface of Mars and analysed the atmosphere and soil.
- **NASA Spirit and Opportunity Rover** is currently investigating Mars.

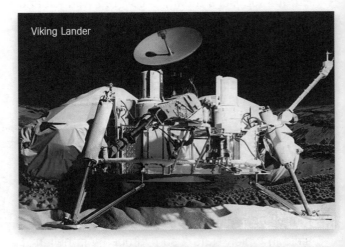

Viking Lander

NASA Spirit and Opportunity Rover

Theories of the Universe

The **Steady State Theory** proposes that the Universe had no beginning and will never end. Few people believe in this theory now.

The **Big Bang Theory** states that the Universe started about 15 billion years ago when a massively dense object experienced a tremendous explosion known as the Big Bang. Since then the Universe has been continually expanding.

There are three theories on the future of the Universe. They all depend upon how much matter there is in the Universe:

1. As the amount of matter increases, gravitational forces will become stronger, slowing the **expansion** of the Universe down and starting to pull the matter back together; this is called the 'big crunch'. There could then be another big bang. This expanding and collapsing Universe is called the **Oscillating Theory**.
2. If there isn't enough matter the Universe will expand forever.
3. If there's just the right amount of matter the Universe will reach a certain fixed size.

Key Words

Big Bang Theory • Dark matter • **Extraterrestrial** • **Oscillating Theory** • **SETI** • **Steady State Theory**

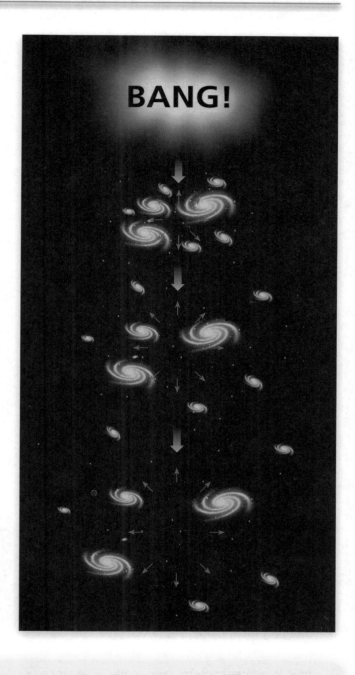

BANG!

HT Dark Matter

All the theories of the Universe depend on an accurate calculation of the mass in the Universe. Scientists have discovered that about 90% of the mass can't be accounted for with known objects like stars and galaxies. This 'missing' mass is called dark matter.

The Hubble Space Telescope has been used to provide detailed images of stars and galaxies, which has helped in the search for dark matter.

Space and its Mysteries

HT Evidence for the Big Bang Theory

Nearby galaxies are 2–3 million light years away (about 20–30 times the diameter of the Milky Way). The majority of galaxies are much further away. Studies of light from these distant galaxies show that galaxies are moving away from us (i.e. the Universe is expanding). Light from these galaxies is 'shifted' towards the red part of the visible spectrum; this is known as red shift.

The blue lines show where some light is absorbed because of elements in the atmosphere. The more distant the solar system, the more it's shifted towards the red end. This shows that the Universe is expanding and that the more distant the galaxy is, the faster it's moving.

Other evidence that supports the Big Bang Theory:

- Large amounts of light elements like hydrogen and helium have been detected throughout the Universe.
- Cosmic microwaves have been detected. These prove that the Universe is cooling (i.e. it started very hot and is cooling as it expands).
- The oldest stars are younger than the Universe.

Increasing distance from Earth

Using Knowledge about the Universe

As a result of space research and exploration, over 1500 useful inventions have been developed. Here are some examples:

- **Imaging technology:** the development of camera microchips for the Hubble telescope led to mobile phone cameras and medical advanced imaging, for example, Digital Image Breast Biopsy and improved ultrasound scanners.
- **Satellite technology:** geostationary communication satellites allow instant news coverage, international telephone calls, the Internet and email. Satellites like Landsat can monitor erosion, deforestation and the temperature of the oceans.

- **Weather forecasting:** satellites like Meteosat give a continuous view of weather fronts so weather can be predicted days in advance.
- Handheld and car navigation systems, as well as intelligence and spy devices, use satellites.
- Smoke detectors, hang gliders, high-powered batteries, sports bras, freeze-dried food, air-traffic control systems and programmable heart pacemakers are all inventions resulting from space exploration.

Key Words

Red shift

Glossary of Key Words

Acceleration – the rate of change of velocity of a body.

Action – a force that's exerted on something.

Asteroid – a piece of rock debris from the asteroid belt between Mars and Jupiter.

Atmosphere – a mass of gases surrounding a planet.

Big Bang Theory – the rapid expansion of material at an extremely high density; the event believed by many scientists to have been the start of the Universe.

Comet – an interplanetary body with a nucleus of dust and ice; has a highly elliptical orbit.

Extraterrestrial – outside the Earth and its atmosphere.

Galaxy – a group of millions of stars held together by gravitational forces.

Gravitational field – the area around an object where gravitational effects are felt.

Gravity – a force that acts between two bodies.

Interplanetary – the area between planets. It contains electromagnetic radiation, solar wind, cosmic rays, microscopic dust particles and magnetic fields.

Mass – a measure of how much matter an object contains.

Nebula – a faint mass of gaseous matter found outside our Solar System.

Orbit – the path that a satellite takes around a larger object (a planet is a satellite of the Sun).

Oscillating Theory – the theory that the expansion of the Universe will eventually slow down and stop, followed by a 'big crunch' with all matter concentrated into a small volume with a very high density, and that the whole process keeps repeating.

Planet – a major body orbiting the Sun or another star.

Radiation – energy in the form of a wave that needs no medium to carry it, e.g. light and radio waves.

Reaction – the equal and opposite of an action force.

SETI – Search for Extraterrestrial Intelligence: a scientific experiment with Internet-connected computers collecting data.

Star – a large gaseous body that radiates light and other electromagnetic radiations and produces energy by nuclear fusion.

Steady State Theory – the theory that the Universe has always existed in a steady state; that it had no beginning and will have no end.

Stellar – relating to a star / stars.

Sun – the star closest to the Earth; the centre of our Solar System.

Temperature – a measure of the relative 'hotness' of a body. It depends upon the average kinetic energy of the particles, measured in °C or K (Kelvin).

Universe – everything that exists as matter and the space in which it's found.

Weight – the gravitational force acting on a body.

Weightlessness – when no weight is felt; where no gravitational force is acting.

HT **Black hole** – a body in the Universe with such a large gravitational strength that even light can't escape; formed at the end of the life cycle of a massive star.

Dark matter – up to 90% of the Universe. Evidence for its existence is measured by gravitational effects rather than by visible observation.

Red shift – light from the distant edges of the Universe is moved (or shifted) towards the red part of the visible spectrum. This shows the Universe is expanding or moving away from the Earth.

Practice Questions

1 Which of the following statements about comets and asteroids are true? Tick the correct options.

    A Comets have a frozen core of gas and dust ◯

    B Asteroids have highly elliptical orbits ◯

    C The tail of a comet is caused by debris being ejected ◯

    D Asteroids are usually found in a band between Mars and Jupiter ◯

2 Choose the correct words from the options given to complete the following sentences.

Jupiter	Solar System	Neptune	Saturn
Sun	lower	higher	

The two largest diameter planets in the _____ are _____

and _____. Their surface temperatures are _____

than the Earth's since they are much further away from the _____.

3 Choose the correct words from the options given to complete the following sentences.

red giant   **supernova**   **white dwarf**   **black hole**   **black dwarf**   **neutron star**

A star the size of the Sun will eventually become a _____before cooling

further and collapsing under its own gravity to become a _____. It will

eventually become a _____.

4 Which of the following statements about gravitational field strength are true? Tick the correct options.

    A It has units of newtons per kilogram (N/kg) ◯

    B It can be calculated using the formula Mass = Weight x Gravitational field strength ◯

    C Acceleration of free-fall has the same value as gravitational field strength ◯

    D Gravitational field strength on the moon is five times that on Earth ◯

HT

5 Which of the following are some of the tests a star must pass before its planets can be classed as potential homes to extraterrestrial life? Tick the correct options.

    A It must be on the main sequence ◯

    B It must have enough light elements (e.g. H, He) to sustain life ◯

    C It must be younger than 4.6 billion years old ◯

    D It must be in the right temperature range ◯

6 Why are unmanned crafts often used in space exploration? Tick the correct options.

   A Because the journeys involve vast distances and times ◯

   B Because they seldom go wrong ◯

   C Because they can't make decisions for themselves ◯

   D Because they are safer to use ◯

HT

7 Choose the correct words from the options given to complete the following sentences.

heavy elements   **main sequence**   **stable conditions**   **right temperature**

To be classed as a potential home for extraterrestrial life, a star must be on the

_____ . It therefore needs to be of the right age and demonstrate

_____ . In addition, it has to be of the _____ and must

have enough of the _____ needed for biological life.

8 Which of the following statements relate to the Big Bang Theory? Tick the correct options.

   A The Universe will expand forever if there isn't enough matter ◯

   B The future of the Universe depends on finding 'dark matter' ◯

   C The expansion may slow down and end up in a 'Big Crunch' ◯

   D The Universe has no beginning or end ◯

9 Which of the following statements are evidence to support the Big Bang Theory? Tick the correct options.

   A The oldest stars are older than the Universe ◯

   B The discovery of cosmic microwaves shows evidence of cooling ◯

   C Light from galaxies is 'red-shifted' in the visible spectrum ◯

   D Lighter elements have not been detected throughout the Universe ◯

10 Choose the correct words from the options given to complete the following sentences.

dark matter   **10%**   **mass**   **90%**   **weight**   **white matter**

The correct theory of the Universe depends on an accurate calculation of the

_____ . About _____ can't be accounted for and this

'missing' amount is called _____ .

Answers to Practice Questions

Environment

1. B
2. B
3. D
4. D
5. **Answer should make reference to:** Natural selection: evolution; over a long period of time; change; survival. Artificial selection: human intervention; individuals selected and bred; over a short period of time.
6. cattle; milk; increased
7. A3; B4; C1; D2
8. **a)** Intensive
   b) Organic
   c) Intensive
   d) Organic

9. **a)–b) Any two from:** Difficult to prove; Many scientists didn't accept it; Contradicted the Bible
10. **a)** **i)–ii) Any two from:** Cold blooded; Gills; Lay eggs in water; Scales.
    b) **i)–ii) Any two from:** Cold blooded; Lungs in adults; Lay eggs in water; Smooth skins.
    c) **i)–ii) Any two from:** Cold blooded; Lungs; Lay eggs; Scaly skins.
    d) **i)–ii) Any two from:** Warm blooded; Lungs; Lay eggs; Feathers.
    e) **i)–ii) Any two from:** Warm blooded; Lungs; Give birth to live young; Fur / hair on skin.

Genes

1. C
2. **a)–b) Any two from:** Faulty genes could be replaced; Ref. to gene therapy; Used in forensics.
3. A3; B2; C4; D1
4. **a)** characteristics; parents; variation; genotype; genes; phenotype.
   b) sexual (reproduction)
5. They have exactly the same genes as the parent.
6. Babies that as embryos have been selected according to their characteristics, e.g. genetic disorders / abnormalities, or sex and cosmetic features.
7. **a)–b) In any order:** Genetics / inheritance; Environment

8. **a)** Gene: part of a chromosome that controls a specific feature; Allele: an alternative form of a gene.
   b) Dominant: the stronger allele in a pair; Recessive: the weaker allele in a pair.
9. A, C, D and F
10. Homozygous: the same alleles in a genetic pair. Heterozygous: different alleles in a genetic pair.
11. R is the gene for roller. r is the gene for non-roller.

	R	R
R	RR	Rr
r	Rr	rr

Electrical & Chemical Signals

1. B
2. D
3. Sensory neurone — Takes nerve impulses from the CNS
   Relay neurone — Passes impulses from one neurone to the next
   Motor neurone — Passes impulses on in the CNS
   Synapse — Takes impulses to the CNS
4. A4; B2; C1; D3
5. A voluntary response is one over which we have control and a reflex response happens automatically.
6. A2; B4; C1; D5; E3
7. The ciliary body relaxes, the suspensory ligaments are pulled tight and the lens is pulled thin.

8. **a)** Transport oxygen
   b) White blood cells
   c) Help to clot the blood
   d) Plasma
9. Oestrogen causes the lining of the uterus to thicken. Progesterone maintains the uterus lining.
10. The pancreas releases insulin. Glucose is converted to glycogen in the liver. Blood glucose levels drop to normal.

Answers to Practice Questions

Use, Misuse & Abuse

1. **a)–c) In any order:** Damage to lungs / liver / brain / kidneys; Cause hallucinations; Slow down reaction times.
2. Alcohol — A substance that alters how the body works
    Caffeine — A drug obtained from opium
    Drug — Pain relief medicine
    Opiate — Fermented liquid that acts as a sedative
    Paracetamol — A stimulant
3. **a)–d) Any four from:** Emphysema; Bronchitis; Chest infections; Cancer; Damaged blood vessels; Heart attacks; Strokes; Arterial disease; Heart disease; Narrowing of blood vessels; Increased blood pressure; Poor oxygen transport by haemoglobin.

4. Stimulants speed up the transmission of nerve impulses. Sedatives slow down the transmission of nerve impulses.
5. C
6. **a)** Direct; horizontal; vertical
    b) Indirect
7. **a)** microbes; a barrier
    b) Cilia; mucus
    c) an enzyme
8. A2; B4; C1; D3
9. Through indirect contact, e.g. coughs / sneezes, bacteria in water droplets, breathed in.
10. **a)–c) In any order:** Toxicity; Safety; Effectiveness / To see if it works.

Patterns in Properties

1. **a)–c) In any order:** Neutrons; Protons; Electrons.
2. The number of protons (or electrons) in one atom of the element.
3. C
4. Exothermic
5. Iron and sulphur
6. $2CuO(s) + C(s) \rightarrow 2Cu(s) + CO_2(g)$
7. He left gaps for undiscovered elements / he was able to work out the atomic mass and properties of undiscovered elements.
8. **a)** Magnesium sulphate
    b) Sodium oxide
9. By looking at its position in the table.

10. B
11. It increases.
12. A precipitation reaction.
13. A, B and D.
14. It's much less dense than air and is non-flammable.
15. The halogens / fluorine, chlorine, iodine, bromine.
16. **a)–b) In any order:** It can kill bacteria so is used in water purification; It is a very good bleach.
17. The iron wool only just glows orange.

Making Changes

1. A1; B4; C3; D2.
2. Reactivity series.
3. B and C.
4. A chemical reaction involving an acid and a base.
5. **a)** Copper sulphate and water.
    b) Calcium chloride, water and carbon dioxide.
6. **a)–c) Any three suitable answers, e.g.:** Fertilisers; Fireworks; Colouring glass, enamels, paints and dyes; As an addition to fuel to improve combustion.
7. Cause other substances to burn more fiercely – Oxidising
    Can cause skin to blister – Irritant
    Attack other materials and living tissue – Corrosive
    Catch fire easily – Flammable
    Can kill – Toxic
8. Natural substances are found in nature and could be harmful. Artificial substances are man-made and less harmful / more reliable.

9. Heat; products; appearance.
10. Carbon dioxide
11. Thermal decomposition
12. The blue copper sulphate becomes dehydrated as water is driven off. The crystals become white anhydrous copper sulphate which will turn back to blue hydrated copper sulphate when the water is added.
13. **a)** **i)–iii) In any order:** Seasoning; Making soap; Chemical production.
    b) **i)–iii) In any order:** Fats; Fabrics; Adhesives.
    c) **i)–iii) In any order:** Preserve food; Condiment; Make plastics.
14. **a)** False
    b) True
    c) True

Answers to Practice Questions

There's One Earth

1. **a)–c) Any three from:** Carbon dioxide is reduced; Nitrogen is produced by bacteria removing nitrates; Carbon from carbon dioxide is locked up in sedimentary rocks; Microorganisms that can't tolerate oxygen are killed off.
2. D
3. Higher levels of greenhouse gases as they prevent heat from leaving the Earth's atmosphere, and cause a rise in the Earth's temperature.
4. A and C
5. **a)–b) Any two from:** Invest in and use new energy technologies that are renewable; Meet the Kyoto protocol; Use geo-engineering for plankton growth.
6. If we are not completely certain about the effects of something, we should act to prevent it.
7. **a)–b) Any two from:** It becomes more viscous; It becomes less flammable; It becomes less volatile; It has a higher boiling point.
8. **a)** **i)–iii) Any three suitable answers, e.g.:** Nitrogen; Oxygen; Carbon dioxide.
   b) Fractional distillation.
9. **a)** plenty.
   b) oxygen; burn; energy.
   c) burns; monoxide.
10. A, D and F.
11. **a)–c) In any order:** Metals; Paper; Glass.
12. Electrolysis of molten sodium chloride.
13. **a)–c) In any order:** Chlorine; Hydrogen; Sodium hydroxide.

Designer Products

1. They change their properties in response to an external stimulus such as heat, light and atmospheric conditions.
2. A unique man-made elastic fibre also known as spandex.
3. After they have been developed.
4. **a)–c) In any order:** Very strong and lightweight; Hard to break; Resistant to chemicals / cutting / fire.
5. A, C and D.
6. They are breathable, lightweight, flexible, warm, soft to the touch and washable.
7. Nanotechnology
8. **a)–d) In any order:** Strength and thermal stability; Flame retardancy; Electrical conductivity and chemical resistance; Decreased permeability to liquids and gases.
9. **Accept any suitable answer, e.g.:** Nanosensors could be used by the military to detect chemical and biological weapons but some people think they could be used to create new threats.
10. By using drip-absorbent sheets to absorb the liquid water or by using humidity buffers to reduce humidity inside the packaging.
11. Fermentation
12. **a)–c) Any three from:** Deficiency in vitamin B causing skin damage, diarrhoea and depression; Decreased levels of iron; Liver damage; Destruction of brain cells; Increased risk of heart disease; Increased risk of high blood pressure.
13. C
14. **a)–c) Any three suitable answers, e.g.:** Bread; Low–fat spreads; Ice-cream; Sponge cakes; Chocolate; Spray cream.

Producing and Measuring Electricity

1. A, B and D
2. 200 hours (hours = capacity / current = 2Ah / 0.01A = 200 hours
3. A, C and D
4. **a)** Resistance = $\dfrac{\text{Voltage}}{\text{Current}}$ = $\dfrac{4V}{0.04A}$ = **100Ω**
   b) Current = $\dfrac{\text{Voltage}}{\text{Resistance}}$ = $\dfrac{4V}{50Ω}$ = 0.08A (not $\dfrac{4V}{150Ω}$)
5. 40V (voltage = current x resistance = 0.2A x 200Ω = 40V
6. B and C
7. different
8. B
9. A, B and C
10. C
11. Maglev (magnetic levitation trains)

You're in Charge

1. B and C
2. A and C
3. **a)** solar cells; sunlight; electricity
   b) watches / calculators; calculators / watches
4. **a)-b) In any order:** Reverses the current direction (every half turn); Keeps the coil rotating (continuously).
5. **a)** car battery **b)** Mains supply. **Accept any other suitable answers.**
6. **a)** efficiency; percentage
   b) power; electrical; watts
7. 3p (Cost = Power x Time x Cost of 1kW = 2kW x 0.2 x 8p = 3p)
8. A, C and D
9. The metal outer case of an appliance must be connected to the earth pin in the plug by the earth wire.
10. **a)** advantage
    b) disadvantage
    c) advantage
    d) advantage
11. A 4; B 2; C 1; D 3; E 5

Answers to Practice Questions

Now You See It, Now You Don't

1. **a)** 3mm
   b) 0.02m (approximately)
   c) 6Hz
   d) 0.12m/s (Wave speed = Frequency x Wavelength = 6Hz x 0.02m = 0.12m/s) (approximately)
2. **a)** Transverse
   b) Longitudinal
   c) Longitudinal
   d) Transverse
3. B, C and D
4. A, C and D
5. **a)** sound
   b) reflected; density
   c) internal
6. Angle of incidence is less than the critical angle – Refraction
   Angle of incidence is greater than the critical angle – Total internal reflection
7. A, C and D
8. **a)** Analogue
   b) Digital
   c) Analogue
   d) Digital
9. A and C

Space and Its Mysteries

1. A and D
2. Solar System; Jupiter; Saturn; lower; Sun.
3. red giant; white dwarf; black dwarf
4. A and C
5. A and D
6. A and D
7. main sequence; stable conditions; right temperature; heavy elements.
8. A, B and C
9. B and C
10. mass; 90%; dark matter.

Notes

Index

Periodic Table

Key

| relative atomic mass |
| **atomic symbol** |
| name |
| atomic (proton) number |

| 1 | | hydrogen | 1 |

Group 1	Group 2											Group 3	Group 4	Group 5	Group 6	Group 7	Group 0
																	4 **He** helium 2
7 **Li** lithium 3	9 **Be** beryllium 4											11 **B** boron 5	12 **C** carbon 6	14 **N** nitrogen 7	16 **O** oxygen 8	19 **F** fluorine 9	20 **Ne** neon 10
23 **Na** sodium 11	24 **Mg** magnesium 12											27 **Al** aluminium 13	28 **Si** silicon 14	31 **P** phosphorus 15	32 **S** sulfur 16	35.5 **Cl** chlorine 17	40 **Ar** argon 18
39 **K** potassium 19	40 **Ca** calcium 20	45 **Sc** scandium 21	48 **Ti** titanium 22	51 **V** vanadium 23	52 **Cr** chromium 24	55 **Mn** manganese 25	56 **Fe** iron 26	59 **Co** cobalt 27	59 **Ni** nickel 28	63.5 **Cu** copper 29	65 **Zn** zinc 30	70 **Ga** gallium 31	73 **Ge** germanium 32	75 **As** arsenic 33	79 **Se** selenium 34	80 **Br** bromine 35	84 **Kr** krypton 36
85 **Rb** rubidium 37	88 **Sr** strontium 38	89 **Y** yttrium 39	91 **Zr** zirconium 40	93 **Nb** niobium 41	96 **Mo** molybdenum 42	[98] **Tc** technetium 43	101 **Ru** ruthenium 44	103 **Rh** rhodium 45	106 **Pd** palladium 46	108 **Ag** silver 47	112 **Cd** cadmium 48	115 **In** indium 49	119 **Sn** tin 50	122 **Sb** antimony 51	128 **Te** tellurium 52	127 **I** iodine 53	131 **Xe** xenon 54
133 **Cs** caesium 55	137 **Ba** barium 56	139 **La*** lanthanum 57	178 **Hf** hafnium 72	181 **Ta** tantalum 73	184 **W** tungsten 74	186 **Re** rhenium 75	190 **Os** osmium 76	192 **Ir** iridium 77	195 **Pt** platinum 78	197 **Au** gold 79	201 **Hg** mercury 80	204 **Tl** thallium 81	207 **Pb** lead 82	209 **Bi** bismuth 83	[209] **Po** polonium 84	[210] **At** astatine 85	[222] **Rn** radon 86
[223] **Fr** francium 87	[226] **Ra** radium 88	[227] **Ac*** actinium 89	[261] **Rf** rutherfordium 104	[262] **Db** dubnium 105	[266] **Sg** seaborgium 106	[264] **Bh** bohrium 107	[277] **Hs** hassium 108	[268] **Mt** meitnerium 109	[271] **Ds** darmstadtium 110	[272] **Rg** roentgenium 111							

Elements with atomic numbers 112–116 have been reported but not fully authenticated

*The lanthanoids (atomic numbers 58–71) and the actinoids (atomic numbers 90–103) have been omitted.

The relative atomic masses of copper and chlorine have not been rounded to the nearest whole number.